THE CONGRESSWOMEN

The Complete Greek Comedy
Edited by William Arrowsmith

Aristophanes

The
Congresswomen
(Ecclesiazusae)

Translated by Douglass Parker
with sketches by Leo and Diane Dillon

Ann Arbor
The University of Michigan Press

Published in the United States of America by
The University of Michigan Press and simultaneously
in Rexdale, Canada, by Ambassador Books Limited

Library of Congress Catalog Card No. 67-14739

Manufactured in the United States of America

S. J. PERELMAN
VIRO ERVDITISSIMO
CVIVS ΛΟΓΟΔΑΙΔΑΛΙΑ ΑΡΙΣΤΟΦΑΝΕΙΑ
VIAM MONSTRAVERAT
HVNC LIBELLVM
DOCTIS PRO DICTIS
INTERPRES
D. D. D.

CONTENTS

Introduction

The Play

The fourth century B.C. was certainly no more than five years old when
a politician named Agyrrhios instituted payment for attendance at
Athens' assembly of the people, the *ecclesia.* It was not much older
when he increased the payment to three obols per man per day. At this
distance, his motives remain obscure; he may simply have been seeking
a solution to the constant problem of pure democracy—how to ensure
a quorum. But at least one pathologist of things democratic took a
darker view. To the playwright Aristophanes, this was one more be-
trayal of the Athenian ideal, one more step toward statism. A legislative
salary was bad enough, but when it approached, however feebly, a
living wage, corruption was sure to follow. Given the normal Athenian
citizen's urge for security, first his livelihood, and then inevitably his
vote, and hence his life, would rest in the hands of demagogues like
Agyrrhios, in hands sure to squeeze. Complete control was just around
the corner, since the assembly was open to every citizen; it was worse
than Kleon and the courts thirty years before.

Kleon's payment of jurors had furnished the occasion for *The Wasps;*
why not do the same for Agyrrhios and the *ecclesia?* Why not demonstrate the implications of this latest constitutional disaster by telescop-
ing its process in a comedy, in which the dithering of a three-obol
assembly would transform the *polis* into something unthinkable over-
night? Why not loot some current Utopian thinking and produce, full-
blown, a totalitarian communistic welfare state? And why not, for that
extra, tested turn of the screw to underscore Athens' current idiocy
and provide manifold chances for comic business—why not have the
takeover of the state masterminded by *women?*

As a correct reconstruction of a playwright's thought processes, the
effusion above is probably as accurate as most other examples of its

1

genre—which is to say, not at all. But, as a presentation of dramatic motive, it seems tolerably close to the facts of the *Ecclesiazusae,* or *The Congresswomen,* which probably attained production in Athens toward the beginning of spring, 392 B.C. Bearded and cloaked, the ladies of Aristophanes' transvestite Chorus pack the assembly, or Congress, and accomplish a coup d'etat patterned closely and avowedly on Agyrrhios' career. Their leader, Praxagora, using ultraconservative arguments to appeal to the voters' desire for stability, rams through a measure which places her and her followers in charge of the entire conduct of the state. Then, uncasing, she reveals herself not only as a woman but as a wild-eyed radical. The program she unfolds to her stunned husband Blepyros is not the implied return to the old virtues, but a completely collective Brave New World marked by community property, community feeding, and community sex. There follows a series of scenes in which bewildered males grapple with these unsettling new realities: Two men (one dutiful, one mean) argue the propriety of turning one's property over to the state, only to have the argument rendered pointless by the announcement of a free dinner. A tense young man, wild to bed his girl, is nearly dismembered by three disgusting crones who lay legal claim to his prior services. Finally, old Blepyros, who has dallied with a brace of dancing girls through the dinner hour, leads the famished Chorus off to the feast, signaling the play's end.

As often in Aristophanes, the "message" supplies impulse and framework without usurping the play itself. In it, the three-obol fee and the communistic Utopia are tied together by congressional decree, but not as principal objects of satire; rather, they constitute a continuum in which we may behold the Athenian cit in his apparently boundless capability for being conned. As for the women, anyone who holds that this is a tract for female emancipation should ponder again Praxagora's equivocation, or the Three Uglies. *The Congresswomen* neither exalts nor demolishes Congress, communism, or women, but mines them for their comic potential. Which makes for awkward pamphleteering, but excellent good comedy. Cast exemplarily, one might say, in normal, bipartite Aristophanic structure: Part One (through Praxagora's program)—achievement of the *tolmêma,* the "Happy Plan"; Part Two—illustration of the Plan's consequences, almost by the numbers, culminating in a happy ending. In summary, a well-knit Old Comedy.

But only in summary. In spite of this almost diagrammatic structure, any full experience of the play leaves one with a sense of discontinuity. Aristophanes seems finally, in middle age, to have justified the criticism often leveled wrongly at *The Acharnians,* his earliest extant play. *The Congresswomen* is broken-backed; the episodes of Part Two, though they illustrate the program of Part One, do not really grow out of it in any meaningful progression, whether of emotion, imagery, or character.

Within scenes, there is a build; within the play as a whole, hardly.

This disconcerting effect derives partly from the evanescent characters. Praxagora, formulator of the Plan, attains her goal and propounds her program . . . and then, with two-fifths of the play remaining, departs the stage, never to return. The reappearance of Blepyros at the end is scarce compensation for this, nor can the efforts of various editors and translators (including this one) to link the two parts with other male characters help very much, since the longest and most striking scene—the trials of the tense young man—contains no character who might have occurred earlier.

Also contributing to the disjuncture is the silence of the Chorus, whose members return victorious from Congress, listen patiently to Praxagora's program . . . and then fall still, uttering not a syllable until they depart at the play's very end. Of course, they *may* have said something in Part Two: The manuscripts twice give the word *XOPOY* there —i.e., "this spot belongs to the Chorus"—which might be the last vestige of lyrics now lost; but it probably indicates no more than wordless dancing. Regardless, our text lacks the choral counterpoint to the action which, in earlier plays, defines and focuses the episodes.

But these shortcomings are symptoms, not freestanding causes; *The Congresswomen's* difficulty lies deeper. A recent critic of Aristophanes has put his finger on the trouble quite by accident, with the observation that this play "has no *agôn* at all." Technically, this is wrong, since the contest or debate known as the *agôn* occurs, admittedly in truncated form, as Praxagora's presentation of her program to the futile objections of Blepyros. But, in a larger sense, the criticism is just: The play lacks, not an *agôn,* but the overarching conflict which the *agôn* normally crystallizes; it possesses no opposition between Chorus and character, and no continuous opposition between character and character. Dramatically, the great potential battle goes by default: We do not actually experience the takeover of Congress, but see the women alone in one-sided rehearsal, while the facts of their victory are conveyed to us more distantly yet, in Chremes' report. The same women make a great to-do about the possibility of their being surprised by some man, but at no time are they ever in any real danger, nor do they even confront a representative male: Blepyros is an easily confused old husband, and nothing more; the tense young man has a universal complaint, but it does not extend beyond his episode. It is this lack of conflict, this lack of fundamental opposition and confrontation, which makes Praxagora leave and the Chorus lie doggo; they have nothing to do. And the play falls apart.

And yet, when all this is said, *The Congresswomen* remains a curiously attractive piece, not great, but fine in its way, and its deficiencies in unity should not blind us to its splayed excellences, which exist in plenty: The sheer technique, at the episodic level, which can arrange routine comic bits into an artistic whole. The wit which can make a long, tough exposition both dramatically and rhetorically meaningful. The verve which can create the longest word in Greek and then use it as a lyric background. The flawless pacing, which can manipulate the cheyne-stokes rhythm of the tense young man's discomfiture so that it restarts with increased wildness just when it seems to have stopped for good. The tact which can somehow maintain the most substantial defecation scene in comedy, or balance a lyric midway between anatomy and bliss.

And, of course, the obscenity itself. Not keeping statistics on such matters, I am unprepared to pronounce *The Congresswomen* Aristophanes' most obscene play; but the dirt, at least in spots, does appear more concentrated than usual. In my view, a concentrated excellence. Not only is it funny, not only is it psychologically right—grasping old Blepyros' anal-retentiveness should bring post-Freudian man up with a start—but, by sheer repeated and varied impact, it transcends disgust and moves on into art. The encounter of the tense young man and the Uglies was frequently censured, in another age not too long ago, as much too long; but shorten it, cut it, and only the shock will remain. Poetry can be made of the strangest materials, and Aristophanes has made it here. A curious excellence, perhaps, and not the most illustrious ornament . . . but a most fitting ornament for this most curious play.

Tastes differ, of course, and I realize that there are those, even in this day and age, who are unwilling to entertain the possibility that the use of obscenity might amount to a positive distinction. I can only wish them well, and hope that they go elsewhere; this play is not for them. There is another type of astigmatism that may be easier to correct— that born of historical perspective. The modern reader of *The Congresswomen* is perhaps uncomfortably aware that the Athenian empire, wellspring and taproot of Western civilization, had crashed into irrevocable ruin a dozen years before. Some critics, obsessed by this knowledge, have let it cloud their vision of playwright and play. To these, it smacks of bad taste and bad form to make fun amid the wreckage; they, therefore, must impugn Aristophanes' skill and sincerity as an artist. One such critic accuses the play of lacking vitality; another marks it the work of an overtired man; a third describes the author as brokenhearted at the cataclysm which had visited his city.

Now, faults *The Congresswomen* has, and they are not to be denied, but nowhere does it give evidence of heartbreak, fatigue, or listlessness. And, as to the charge of laughing in the ruins—well, the participants in a cataclysm are often the last to know. Aristophanes, like most other inhabitants of an Athens still busily combining against Sparta, had not heard the crash.

Translation

The principles governing this translation into American English remain those enunciated in the Introductions to my versions of *The Acharnians, The Wasps,* and *Lysistrata,* to which the reader is referred. There has been one slight change in orientation, however, which should be set down here: In making my earlier translations, I hoped for production without really expecting it; on looking back, I seem often to have aimed for a theater in the reader's head rather than one before his eyes. Stage directions overflowed, explanatory expansions of the text often slowed down pace, rhetoric swelled in compensation for the lack of physical production. These days, however, such production is becoming more and more usual. I don't regret my former practice; any good director knows when to cut. But in translating *The Congresswomen* I have had more of an eye to an actual stage and the problems of immediate apprehension by an audience, and may thus have assimilated the obscure to the familiar, or suppressed proper names, rather more often than formerly. I have tried to rectify such actions in the Notes, but the dedicated antiquary will do well to check the Greek.

Text

Most plays of Aristophanes cry aloud for new editions; the *Ecclesiazusae* shrieks, since its Greek text has normally been edited only to fill out the set. (In all the extant plays of Aristophanes it is occasionally difficult to tell who speaks a given line; in this play it is all too frequently impossible to say with any certainty who is in the cast.) I have done what I could with the best available text, that of Coulon (1930), bolstering it with the editions of Rogers (1916) and Van Leeuwen (1905). Major departures from Coulon's text are indicated in the Notes.

Acknowledgments

This translation was made while I was a fellow of the University of California's Institute for the Creative Arts, and I take this opportunity to express my gratitude and thanks. Also, to William Arrowsmith, my thanks for trust and tutelage. To my wife Haverly, my thanks for trust, encouragement, and endurance throughout the vagaries of an English spring.

DOUGLASS PARKER

Characters of the Play

PRAXAGORA, *an Athenian woman of somewhat radical views*

FIRST WOMAN

SECOND WOMAN

THIRD WOMAN

FIRST KORYPHAIA

SECOND KORYPHAIA

CHORUS OF ATHENIAN WOMEN

PHEIDOLOS, *a mean man*

BLEPYROS, *a suspicious man and part-time barrator, husband to Praxagora*

CHREMES, *a dutiful man*

A CRIERESS

A HAG

A SWEET YOUNG THING

EPIGENES, *a tense young man*

A CRONE

A HARRIDAN

ASSORTED WOMEN AND SLAVES

SCENE: *A street in Athens, on which front three houses.* These are, at the moment, allotted thus: House I, center, Praxagora and her husband Blepyros; House II, stage left, the Second Woman and her husband Pheidolos; House III, stage right, Chremes. The time is early morning; it is still dark. Praxagora emerges stealthily from House I. She wears a long cloak and red slippers, and carries, in one hand, some wreaths, a staff, and a long false beard. The other hand contains a large clay lamp, lit. After a cautious look around, she puts down wreaths, staff, and beard, strides purposefully forward, and mock-tragically begins what seems to be an invocation of the sun* filched from a Euripidean prologue.*

PRAXAGORA
O beam resplendent,
                    blaze of glazèd gaze,
O horribly gorgeous orb, who wheeled and sprang,
the fairest ware of those who live for the kiln,
Raising the lamp in both hands.
O Bedside Lamp . . .
                    (I really feel I should
divulge your parentage and fate; you've come so far
from low beginnings.)
                    Earth thou wert, but spun
to life and tried in the furnace, you quitted the potter's
field for higher pastures, and now your nasal
orifices spurt forth the Sun's effulgent
offices.
                    Therefore, Lamp, impel abroad
the supersecret signals we have fixed.
She waves the lamp vigorously.
You're the only nonwoman who knows our code;
you've earned our trust.
                    When we, within our rooms,
strain and struggle to rehearse new shapes of love,
in closest intercourse you guard our flanks.
And when we splay our bodies in supine display,
you oversee the action from the rear, an eye inside
the house whom no one shuts or closes out.
Your shaft alone is privy to our inmost nooks,
and privately in those parts its burning glance
defoliates unwanted hair. Or, when from the well-stocked

cellar we sneak away the yield and stream
of Bakchos, you are there, O friend and guide,
O faithful accomplice, never known to spill
a word to the neighbors.

                Wherefore, friend, you now
shall be apprised, at nearest hand, of all
*decisions taken and actions passed last summer**
by my assembled associates.

                —Except, there's no one
here. They should have come. It's getting on
toward dawn. The Congress* takes up any minute now,
and we've got to get seats . . .

Realizing, with a start, that she has dropped the
paratragic rhetoric.

                oh, pardon me; forgot . . .
We must dispone our limbs in crafty slyness
on what the noted spoonerizer Phyromachos
once deigned to name those beery wenches.*

                —But what
could the trouble be? They couldn't follow directions
and sew their beards on? It was too much of a task
for them to snaffle their husbands' cloaks and not
get caught?

She looks off right.

             Oh, there's a lamp. It's coming this way.
I'd better beat a retreat. With the luck I'm having,
this visitor might turn out to be a Man.

She takes up a position beside House I. Shortly, a
gaggle of women, who will later group and form as
the First Semichorus, straggles on from the right.
They bear (and in some cases wear) men's cloaks,
shoes, canes, and beards. Leading them is the First
Woman, who is earnestly trying to counterfeit
maleness.

FIRST WOMAN

Time to be on the march, men. While we were assembling,
the second reveille blew. Two cocks and a doodle.

PRAXAGORA

Stepping forward.

            Do tell. And I was reveling here in an all-night
wait for you.

              But just a moment. Let me
summon my neighbor. Just a scratch at her door;
she'll be in a scrape if her husband hears.

She taps lightly at the door of House II, which
is immediately opened by the Second Woman.

SECOND WOMAN

Enough.

I heard your nails. Just putting on my shoes.
Not that I had a single wink of sleep.
Never marry a sailor, darling. Always
fumbling around in the stern sheets, catching me
right between wind and water . . . I had to double
the cape all night before I could snitch this cloak.

PRAXAGORA

Looking off left, where a second muddled and motley
group of women, who will form, eventually, the
Second Semichorus, is beginning to enter. They are
led, or better preceded, by the Third Woman.

Well, now. Here comes Kleináretê—better late
than never—that one must be Sóstratê, and there's
Philaínetê.

THIRD WOMAN

To the stragglers.

Better get a move on! Glykê laid us
under an oath: The last one there picks up
the tab for three gallons of wine and a peck of cockles.

SECOND WOMAN

Look, here's Melístichê, slogging along in Smikýthion's
clogs.

PRAXAGORA

Why such a mad dash? With a man like hers,
she had all night to get here.

FIRST WOMAN

Geusístratê's got
a torch. That means lights out in her husband's bar.

PRAXAGORA

Here's Philodorétos' wife, and Mrs. Chairétades. . .
and here come loads of others, perfect crowds
of the very best women—Athens' complete elite!

THIRD WOMAN

Arriving before Praxagora.

Had the godawfullest trouble getting away,
darling. My husband was at it all night.

PRAXAGORA

At it

all night?

THIRD WOMAN

Yes, the pig. He stuffed himself
on sardines at supper and couldn't sleep for burping.

PRAXAGORA
Very well. Be seated.

Now that I've got you together,
I'd like to run a check on your performance.
Have you complied completely with all the directives
we drafted and passed at Athene's feast last summer?

FIRST WOMAN
I certainly have. First, as per understanding,
I let my underarms bush up into jungles.
Next, every time my husband went downtown,
I smeared my body with oil and spent the day
standing in the sun and getting an allover tan.

SECOND WOMAN
Me, too. I started by slinging my razor right out
of the house, and now I'm such a mass of fuzz
I don't even look like a woman any more.
Well, not to a casual glance.

PRAXAGORA

Another point
in the compact. We each agreed to bring a beard
to this meeting. Do you have yours?

THIRD WOMAN
Producing her false beard.

Mine's divine!

SECOND WOMAN
Producing a huge beard.

And mine's in line with fashion. Epikrates decrees
that this year's beardline's below the knees.

PRAXAGORA
To the crowd of women.

Do you

have yours?

FIRST WOMAN

Boy, do they. Look at those hairy nods.

PRAXAGORA

Well, everything else appears to be in order.
Let's see, now. Slippers, check. And ditto the canes.
And ditto your husbands' cloaks.

Just as agreed.

FIRST WOMAN

Producing a tremendous club.

I stole this cane from my husband while he was sleeping.
As usual.

PRAXAGORA

Just what does your husband *do*?

FIRST WOMAN

Delivers

logs. You know him—Lamios.*

SECOND WOMAN

Oh, yes—the man

who lets those tremendous farts!

FIRST WOMAN

It's such a waste

of talent: He carries a big stick, farts like an army . . .
If only he could stay awake, he'd make
a fortune in politics.

PRAXAGORA

And now, before the stars

decide to leave the sky, we'd better decide
on our next move. We've made all these preparations
to go to Congress, and Congress takes up at dawn.

FIRST WOMAN

God, yes. You'll have to get us over there early;
we want those seats down front by the speaker's stand,
facing the Executive Board.

THIRD WOMAN

Holding up a large phallos.

See what I brought.

PRAXAGORA

What's that?

THIRD WOMAN

A carding comb. I thought I could work

the snaggles out of my wool until the men
started Congress in earnest.

PRAXAGORA

What's the point,
you nitwit?

THIRD WOMAN

I'm sure there's bound to be some connection . . .
and anyway, I can listen just as well
while I flog away at my fleece.

I *have* to do it.
My kids are positively *nude*.

PRAXAGORA

That's all we need.
Card your wool, indeed. *No man must see
the slightest bit of your body.*

We've got to hurry;
the littlest slip and we're undone. I can see it all:
The people assemble, Congress commences . . . and then
we arrive in a flap, some woman climbs over a bench,
flips up her cloak, and exposes, to all and sundry,
some misplaced whiskers.

But if we get there first
and take our places, we can adjust our clothing
and no one'll be the wiser. And once we're there,
with proper beards tied on and arranged in place,
what casual observer will say that we're not men?

FIRST WOMAN*
You're right. Agyrrhios started out as a woman,
but then he stole a fluteplayer's beard, and pulled
the wool over everyone's eyes, and look at him now:
He runs the city.

PRAXAGORA

And Agyrrhios, girls, is our model.
By the gods of daylight robbery, let's try to pull
a *coup* as big as his. Let's devise a device
to take command, take charge, take over. *We'll* run
the city, run it right and proper and well.
No more sitting and drifting in a ship of state
with empty oarlocks and barren masts!

THIRD WOMAN

Now, look:
We're *women*! What place is there on the floor of Congress
for feminine intercourse? How can we fit in?

14

PRAXAGORA

You'd be surprised. It's agreed that the most persuasive
speakers are smoothskinned, softvoiced boys who've been screwed
to a pitch of eloquence—and *that* is a qualification
that we possess in plenty.

THIRD WOMAN

That may be okay
for rump sessions, but what's our official position? The thing
we lack is practice.

PRAXAGORA

And that, in case you've forgotten,
is precisely why we're here—to rehearse our speeches.
Now hurry and get that beard tied on.
The same
for those of you who've been practicing how to talk.

SECOND WOMAN

You mean there's someone here who doesn't know how?

PRAXAGORA

You tie your beard on. Quickly. Be a man.
I'll set these wreaths down here and put mine on
with the rest of you. I just might want to speak.

*All the women adjust their beards. The Second
Woman, still beard-proud, points at the women
before her.*

SECOND WOMAN

Praxagora, honey, look over here. The funniest
thing I ever saw.

PRAXAGORA

The funniest? How?

SECOND WOMAN

That fringe
around their chins. They look like roasted squids.

PRAXAGORA

As a herald.

*Attention, please! The ritual purification will now
commence. The Chaplain will pass among you, bearing
the sacrificial polecat.*

FIRST WOMAN

I thought they sacrificed pigs.

PRAXAGORA

We couldn't get a pig.

15

FIRST WOMAN

But why a polecat?

SECOND WOMAN

It gives an odor of holiness.

PRAXAGORA

Move down front!

As if to an inattentive member of Congress.
(Ariphrades, hold your tongue. Come up and sit down.)
—Who wishes to address the assembled Congress?

SECOND WOMAN

I do.

PRAXAGORA

Wear this wreath on your brow.* May fortune attend you.

SECOND WOMAN

Adjusting the wreath.

This look all right?

PRAXAGORA

You may proceed to speak.

SECOND WOMAN

Before I've had a drink?

PRAXAGORA

What drink do you mean?

SECOND WOMAN

Well, isn't this party politics?

PRAXAGORA

Yes . . .

SECOND WOMAN

So where's

the party?

PRAXAGORA

Snatching back the wreath.

Get out of here. A fat lot of help
you'd be up there.

SECOND WOMAN

You mean they *don't* drink in Congress?

PRAXAGORA

Of all the fatuous questions . . .

17

SECOND WOMAN

They do *too* drink—
what's more, they drink it straight. They pass decrees
that sound just like D.T.s.

FIRST WOMAN

She's right. They pour
libations, too. I know they do: They're always
praying, and prayers without wine are perfectly pointless.

THIRD WOMAN

And the language. They slander each other like men on benders,
and then the police come along and sling out the drunks.

PRAXAGORA

Move along and sit down. You're worse than useless.

SECOND WOMAN

I wish to god I'd never grown a beard.
This thing absorbs saliva. I'm positively parched.

PRAXAGORA

Is anyone else desirous of speaking?

FIRST WOMAN

I am.

PRAXAGORA

Then get this wreath on. Don't hold up the agenda.
Give us a firmly grounded masculine speech . . .
and don't fall over. Use your cane for support.

FIRST WOMAN

Unaccustomed as I am, I would have preferred
to yield the floor to some more experienced speaker.
But since I have risen, I cannot refuse to attach
a widespread abuse in this city. I refer, of course,
to Corruption at the Bar. Does anyone realize
how many cases there are in Athens' taverns
filled up with water? Heavens to Betsy,* it isn't . . .

PRAXAGORA

Heavens to Betsy, deadhead? Where did you leave
your brain?

FIRST WOMAN

What's wrong? I didn't ask for a drink.

PRAXAGORA

No, but what man swears by *Heavens to Betsy?*
The rest was beautifully stated. Right to the point.

18

FIRST WOMAN

Oh.

Back into the speech.

—GODDAM IT ALL, it . . .

PRAXAGORA

Snatching back the wreath.

Stop. Enough.

Now get this straight: I won't take another step
toward commandeering Congress unless the strictest accuracy
is observed in everything we do.

SECOND WOMAN

Running back up to Praxagora.

Give me the wreath.

I want another chance to speak. I know
I've got it right this time. All practiced and everything.

Putting on the wreath and striking an attitude.

—It is my pleasure to address you, girls . . .

PRAXAGORA

Snatching back the wreath.

The same mistake again. These are not girls,
they're MEN.

SECOND WOMAN

Pointing to the audience.

It's Epigonos' fault. I saw him sitting
out there and thought I was talking to women.

PRAXAGORA

Scat.

To First Woman.

You too.

To First, Second, and Third Women.

Now sit down over there. You force me
to a hard decision: I'll do the speaking myself.
But first, the wreath.

She puts it on.

I pray the gods will direct
today's deliberations to some successful issue.

A pause, and she begins a formal address.

—My friends: I bear a share no less than yours
in this land of ours, and feel compelled to confess
to a mounting distress. In fact, my grief is great
at the state of our City: Something is rotten in Athens.
Our leaders, our elected officials, are routinely vicious;
if one steps out of line and delivers a day

of honest performance, he balances this with a week
of corruption. Give the job to another, he plumbs
yet deeper depths of depravity. All this indicates
your senselessly finical nature, which makes me despair
of giving you any advice. Your standard behavior
to prospective friends is frightened rejection, the while
you go on your knees to woo potential enemies.
It shakes my faith in government: A few years back,
we never convened the Congress at all, but we knew
one thing for certain: we all agreed Agyrrhios
was a crook.

              But then this crook established a salary
for legislative attendance. So now we convene the Congress . . .
and those of us who get paid are loud in his praise,
while those of us who don't are equally loud
in demanding death for those who pass laws for money.

FIRST WOMAN
Goodness gracious, what a lovely speech!

PRAXAGORA
—Can't you stop that harebrained swearing? *Goodness
gracious* . . . that would sound just peachy in Congress.

FIRST WOMAN
I wouldn't say it there.

PRAXAGORA
                    Don't get the habit.
Back to the speech.
           —Or take the current Alliance against the Spartans: *
During debate, it was roundly affirmed that Athens'
future depended upon it; alliance or ruin.
But once we voted it in and the League was established,
reaction arose with a vengeance, so savage and swift
that the man who'd maneuvered acceptance of the longed-for
    League
had to leg it out of the city or lose his life.
—I turn to your wishy-washy stand on seapower:
Should Athens launch a fighting navy?* The poor man
thinks of pay, and votes YES; the rich man thinks
of tax, and votes NO; the farm bloc thinks of reprisals,
and joins the rich man.
                  —And Korinth: Only yesterday
you detested Korinth, and Korinth detested you.
Today they're friends and allies; therefore, play
along, about face, be friends and allies too. . . .

The polymath hasn't a brain in his head; the mangiest
moron in town is sporting the name of Sage.
Whoops, there went a glimpse of Salvation . . . but no,
the savior's out of bounds, and nobody calls.*

SECOND WOMAN
This man is profound.

PRAXAGORA
                   (Now, there is proper praise.)
—Of all this higgledypiggledy mixture of moral
incertitude you stand guilty, people of Athens.
You draw a public wage for serving in Congress
with blinders which narrow each man's vision to private
profit, while General Welfare wobbles along
like a drunken cripple.
                   However, All is Not Lost:
Give me your support, and you may yet be saved.
I here propose that we relinquish the State
to a trained managerial class, trustees and directors
of our happy homes—to our wives and daughters—in short,
to the *Women*.

WOMEN
          Hurray!
              —Hurrah!
                   —Huzzah!
                       —Hear! Hear!

PRAXAGORA
The superior nature of the female's behavior pattern
to that of the common male like you or me
is easily shown. Example: Every girl jill
of those women washes her wool in hot water, just like
her mother before her; you never catch them casting
about for a newfangled method.
                   But male-run Athens
has always been *in* hot water, for just the opposite
reason: We men can never resist improving
on something that works; we tinker and innovate the City
right into the ground. Not so the women. Women
are truly conventional, natural-born conservatives:
             Women kneel to bake their bread,
             tote their laundry on the head,
               —just like Mother.
            Trust a tested recipe,

Keep Demeter's yearly spree,*
   —just like Mother.
Nag their husbands till they're dead,
hide their lovers under the bed,
   —just like Mother.
Pad the grocery bill with snacks,
take a drink or three to relax,
prefer their pleasure on their backs,
happy nymphomaniacs,
   —just like Mother.
Therefore, gentlemen, why waste time in debate?
Why deliberate possible courses of action?
Simply hand over the City and let the women
rule. You need convincing? Reflect: Mothers
all, their first desire will be to preserve
their soldier sons.

       Provisions? Who quicker than
the hand that rocks the cradle at filling the mouth?
Finances? Nothing more wily than women at scrounging
a budget—and rest assured that, once in power.
they won't allow embezzlement of public funds;
by dint of training, they themselves are Athens'
finest embezzlers.

       I say no more. Give me
your support, and vote yourselves a life of bliss.

FIRST WOMAN
Lovely, Praxagora darling. Right on the button.

SECOND WOMAN
But where did you learn to talk so beautifully, baby?

PRAXAGORA
During the Terror,* my husband and I hid out
on the Pnyx, where Congress meets. Got lost in the crowd,
and listened to politicians. Learned them all by heart.

FIRST WOMAN
I'm not surprised. You're simply fiendishly clever.
If you can manage to bring your project off,
we'll elect you commander-in-chief on the spot.

THIRD WOMAN
                  But what
if Kephalos starts—worse luck—to call you names?
Can you counter attacks from him in open debate?

PRAXAGORA
I'll say he's deranged.

THIRD WOMAN
So what? Everyone knows that.

PRAXAGORA
A manic-depressive, downhill phase.

THIRD WOMAN
That won't
faze him. Everyone knows that, too.

PRAXAGORA
I'll say
that a man who turns out such tasteless vases would surely
make Athens go to pot.

SECOND WOMAN
But suppose Neokleides
squints his bleary eyes and begins to get nasty?

PRAXAGORA
I'll tell him that sight like his is better suited
for an open-ended probe of a diarrheic dog.

FIRST WOMAN
The members may rise to a point of order. Won't that
stop your flow?

PRAXAGORA
I'm sure I can handle their points.
I have a penchant for twisting things.

FIRST WOMAN
A what?

PRAXAGORA
A knack.

SECOND WOMAN
There's only one danger left. Suppose
the police start dragging you out in the middle—what
can you do?

PRAXAGORA
I'll put my hands on my hips. That way,
my middle is always safe; they'll have to try
for my end.

THIRD WOMAN
We won't sit idle. If they make any
attempt to pick you up, we'll shout them down.

FIRST WOMAN

I think we've got together on a marvelous plan,
but there's still one technical point we haven't worked out.
It's Voting: I know they record their votes by waving
their hands, but how? The only practice we've had
is spreading our legs.

PRAXAGORA

It isn't an easy procedure;
requires some effort.

Demonstrating.

First, the right-hand sleeve
is grasped in the left hand, and then shoved back, exposing
the shoulder. The freed right arm is then raised stiffly,
thus.

That's it.

To the whole crowd of women.

Now tuck up your dresses. High.
Then on with those Spartan go-to-meeting shoes. And tie
them tight, the way your husband does whenever
he's ready to go to Congress—or wherever else
he says he's going. When this is all in perfect
order, fasten up the beards. Be fussy. Make sure
the adjustment is right in line.

Next thing, put on
those overcloaks you stole from your men this morning.
Around the shoulders, so.

And now the canes.
You lean on these when you walk. And while you walk,
you sing. Some antique, elderly melody. Try
to sound like old men tottering in from the country.

FIRST WOMAN

That's beautifully put. But as for us, we'd better
rush on ahead and intercept the girls who are really
coming in from the country. They'll probably go
direct to the Pnyx.

PRAXAGORA

Then hurry. The rule up there
is In by Dawn, or No Pay. The man who isn't
abreast of the times slinks home without a tittle.

*She exits quickly left, followed by the First,
Second, and Third Women. The remaining women,
fully disguised, are grouped into formation as First
and Second Semichoruses by the First and
Second Koryphaiai.*

FIRST KORYPHAIA
>Time to commence
>our journey, gents,
>and "gents" is the magic word.
>>The slightest blunder
>>will send us under;
>don't let your gender get blurred.
>>Our beautiful plot
>>will come to naught
>if you expose your sex;
>>>so, girls, be male
>>>and don't let's fail
>unmanned by some damned reflex.

FIRST SEMICHORUS
Singing as they start off.

>To Congress, gentlemen. On our way.
>>to make our country's laws.
>The pay's three obols per man per day
>>but we've got troubles, because:

>>>The authorities state
>>>that the going rate
>>>will only apply
>>>to the sour-faced guy
>>>who arrives half-dead,
>>>unwashed and unfed,
>>>by dawn's early light
>>>just past midnight . . .
>>>*He* gets his fee;
>>>come later, vote free.

>So keep up, Drákês and Smíkythos,
>>while we rehearse our vote.
>Come on, Charitímidês, follow close;
>>we're dead if there's one false note.

>>>First, we'll check in
>>>before they begin;
>>>next, down we'll flock
>>>and get seats en bloc;
>>>then one of us will
>>>propose a bill
>>>in which we'll concur
>>>and vote for her . . .

A shocked pause.

> Now, there's a gaffe that could be grim:
> Correction, please: we'll vote for *him*.

They move off toward the left, followed by the
Second Semichorus, whose members have cast
themselves as men from the countryside.*

SECOND SEMICHORUS

> Let's shove these townies out of the way.
> This order's preposterous:
> No johnny-come-latelies who vote for pay
> can crowd ahead of *us*.

> When we drew one obol,
> it was too much trouble
> for them to attend;
> they'd chin with a friend
> in the market, and let
> the rest of us sweat
> out the vote. But these days,
> since the recent raise,
> they clog the queue,
> and we can't get through.

> In the golden days of Myrónidês,
> Athens had better men.
> Nobody dreamed of demanding fees
> for being a citizen.

> For statesmanship
> the reward was a sip
> of wine, plus a few
> ripe olives, say two
> small onions, a dried-
> out crust . . . supplied
> at your own expense.
> But that's long since:
> Now Congress is commerce, and politics
> pays just as well as hauling bricks.

They follow the First Semichorus off left.
A pause, and the door of House II opens. Pheidolos
appears, in misery. He wears a skimpy woman's
shift and gaudy house slippers a number of
sizes too small, and walks cramped.

26

PHEIDOLOS*
What the hell is happening here? It's nearly
sunup, and where's my wife? Disappeared without trace.
She's gone, my clogs are gone, my cloak is gone
and me . . . oooh god, I gotta go. For the last
three hundred years I've been lying in bed, expanding,
trying to find some clothes so I could answer
the hammering at my back door. But Peristalsis won't wait.
I had to settle for this slip of my wife's, and scuff
her Persian mules on over my toes.

He looks around.

                                        Oh, hell.
Damn built-up area. Where's a suitable spot
to shit?
                        But it's still dark out. Who's to see?
Any old spot'll suit me.

*He squats, center stage. The door to House I
opens, and old Blepyros appears, in the same
agony and a different costume. He wears a saffron-
colored shrug over his shoulders, and wobbles
precariously along in Praxagora's wedgies.*

BLEPYROS
                                Goddamitt, OWWW!
I ought to be taken out and flayed alive
for getting married at my age. Don't know what
my wife sneaked out to do, but it's nothing healthy.
Still, on we go. My bowels can't wait on her.

*As yet unnoticed by Pheidolos, he stumbles to center
stage and squats, facing the other way. They
remain there, back to back, for a moment,
then Pheidolos turns.*

PHEIDOLOS
Who's this? My next-door neighbor Blepyros?

BLEPYROS
                                                God, yes.
The very same.

PHEIDOLOS
                        What's all that yellow on your shoulders?
Don't tell me Kinesias missed the head again?*

BLEPYROS
How's that? Oh, no. This thing's my wife's. Her shrug.
I had to put something on to come out. She usually
wears it.

PHEIDOLOS
    Where's your cloak?

BLEPYROS
                       I couldn't say.
I looked all through the covers for it. No luck.

PHEIDOLOS
You didn't ask your wife where it was?

BLEPYROS
                           I didn't;
no wife in there to ask. She must have bored
her way out while I was asleep. It doesn't augur
well for the future. She's up to something. Something
radical.

PHEIDOLOS
      Dammit, that's just what happened to me.
My better half took the cloak right off me and left.
Not that I minded that, but she lifted my clogs
as well. At least, I couldn't find them. I'm shoeless.

BLEPYROS
Well, what do you know? So'm I. My go-to-meeting shoes
are gone; the ones I always wear to Congress.
But I had to go, so I wormed her wedgies on
and wobbled out here. It was either that or let it
fly in the nice clean sheets.

PHEIDOLOS
               But what could it be?
Did one of her girlfriends ask her over to breakfast?

BLEPYROS
I'm sure that's it. No hanky-panky from her.
My wife's no whore.
               As far as I know.

PHEIDOLOS
*Rising and gazing down at Blepyros, who
remains squatting.*

                   You must
be squeezing out a hawser, instead of shit.
It's time for me to get to Congress. Provided
I locate that cloak. My only one.

BLEPYROS

I'm going
to Congress, too, if I ever finish here.
I ate an unripe plum, and it's jammed the passage.
My food's cut off.

PHEIDOLOS

And pressing your rear. A late
dispatch from the front.*

BLEPYROS

You said it; a steady build-up,
restricting freedom of movement.

Pheidolos exits into House II.

So what do I do?
Is there no way out? The stoppage is only starting;
what's next? Presuming I keep on eating, where
do I fit the shit? Some green plumber's plugged
my fixtures, and no relief in sight.

To the audience.

—Pardon.
Can some one fetch a physician?

(But what physician?
It's rather a narrow specialty.)

Is there a practicing
homosexual here who's free at the moment? Maybe
Amynon?

(But he won't come. It's not his end
of the business.)

Antisthenes! That's who I want. A man
who grunts like that can feel what constipation means;
he's always making an ass of himself.

Pause for a reply which does not come.

No luck?

Still squatting, he raises his arms toward heaven.

—Goddess of childbirth, grant my labor some issue
quickly, before I split. Oh, render me corkless
before they stick me under the bed as a comic
prop. My mother didn't raise her boy
to be emptied by hand.

*A minor explosion, coinciding with the entrance,
left, of Chremes, who starts to cross to House III,
but stops when he sees Blepyros.*

CHREMES

Can you be taking a crap?

BLEPYROS

Straightening up hurriedly.

Who, me? No more, thank god. Relief at last.

CHREMES

Enchanting costume for it. Your wife's?

BLEPYROS

It was dark

inside the house. I had to take what I got.
And now give me a straight answer: Where've you been?

CHREMES

To Congress.

BLEPYROS

Adjourned already?

CHREMES

Right on the dot

of dawn.

BLEPYROS

That's early.

CHREMES

It is. And oh, the ridiculous

mess they made in rounding up a quorum.

BLEPYROS

You got your pay—three obols?

CHREMES

I wish I had.

This time I came too late. I'm so embarrassed.

BLEPYROS

Ashamed to be late?

CHREMES

Financially embarrassed. I'm broke.

BLEPYROS

But why were you late?

CHREMES

I couldn't get in. The place

was jammed—the biggest crowd since they opened the Pnyx.
A curious bunch. The consensus was, they were cobblers.

BLEPYROS

Cobblers?

CHREMES

They all had that pasty complexion that comes
from indoor labor. Congress appeared to be packed
with anemia victims. Which made me a gratis voter,
me and lots of others.

BLEPYROS

No chance for me
to get paid if I get there now?

CHREMES

No chance for you
if you got there *then*—unless you beat the second
crow of the cock.

BLEPYROS

*Mock-tragic, taking off Achilles' reaction at
Patroklos' death in Aischylos' tragedy* The Myrmidons.

What bitter blow is this?
Raise not the dirge for dead, departed money;
'Tis I who now must drag out a cashless existence;
O sweet Antilochos, raise the ante for me!
—But what made such a mob assemble so early?

CHREMES

The Executive Board decided to put the question
of Public Safety to a popular vote. Straight off
Neokleides, the local glaucoma king, was trying
to sneak up to speak up first. This raised a general
shout, as you might imagine:
"What a revolting
sight—a man who can't keep his lashes apart
is trying to prescribe a method to hold the State
together." He bleared through the film, and squinted around,
then raised a shout of his own:
"Inform me, friends,
what *is* the remedy?"

BLEPYROS

"A clove of garlic pounded
in an ounce of vinegar; mix in the juice of one Spartan
milkweed; apply the mess to your eyelids at night"—
that's what I'd have told him. If I'd been there.

CHREMES

Euaion was next—a masterful, versatile speaker,
known for his unadorned manner. Came on completely
nude. Or so it appeared; he claimed he was wearing

a cloak. His address was loaded to the lip with appeal:
"Friends," said he, "my obvious lack of savings—
a mere five hundred obols would set me right—
should not disqualify me from showing you
the way toward saving the city and people of Athens.
When winter comes, collect the needy—all those
who get caught short when the nights get long—and take them
to the cleaners.
                    And make the cleaners give each one
a woolen cloak off the racks. That way, we'll be saved
from pneumonia. Then, those without beds and covers—save them
a place to sleep after dinner, in the tanners' shops.
And if any tanner locks his door in the winter,
the state will have his hide . . . three hides, in fact,
with the hair left on."

BLEPYROS
                    An excellent blanket proposal.
No man would have raised a hand against him, if only
he'd added this: "The Wheat Exchange* will donate dinner—
a peck per pauper per day—or else be soundly
thrashed." One way to make a present profit
from dealers in futures.

CHREMES
                    A handsome fellow spoke next,
quite young. And pale—he looked like Nikias does.

BLEPYROS
But *he's* been dead for years.*

CHREMES
                    I said the boy
was pale. He jumped up front and began to harangue us.
Insisted our only salvation was placing the state
in the hands of the women. That mob of cobblers applauded
and screamed, Hear, Hear.
                    It didn't sit well with the farm bloc,
though. They set up a rumble.

BLEPYROS
                    Thus showing brains.

CHREMES
But lacking volume; the young man drowned them out.
He recited a lengthy list of female virtues,
and balanced each one with a vice. To be precise,
a vice of yours.

BLEPYROS

        So what did he say?

CHREMES

                          Well, first

he called you a shyster . . .

BLEPYROS

            Not you?

CHREMES

                      Please don't interrupt.

And then a gangster . . .

BLEPYROS

          Just me?

CHREMES

                  As Zeus is my judge.

And further, a fink.

BLEPYROS

         Just me?

CHREMES

                As Zeus is my judge . . .

Pointing to the audience.

just you and that mob out there.

BLEPYROS

                So what else is new?

CHREMES

But woman, he claimed, is a far superior being,
glutted with judgment, productive of profit in plenty . . .
and buttoned on the lip. The yearly female festivals
preserve unbreached security, but when you and I
serve in the Senate, it's raining classified matter
all over town.

BLEPYROS

        By Hermes, God of Liars,

that's true.

CHREMES

        Then women, he said, are always lending
each other something—dresses, accessories, cash,
or cups; completely private loans, with never
a witness around—and every item's returned,
no hint of fraud. While most men tend, he claimed,
to filch from their friends.

34

BLEPYROS

                      By Poseidon, God of Welshers,
in front of ever so many witnesses, yet.

CHREMES

According to him, the women don't lodge complaints,
or prosecute suits, or plot to destroy democracy;
instead, they bring boundless boons, and bounties, and whatever's
good. He went on for a while, but that was his gist.

BLEPYROS

And how did we vote?

CHREMES

                To entrust the city to women.
By general agreement, that was the only scheme
that Athens had missed.

BLEPYROS

                  And that's the vote?

CHREMES

                          The law.

BLEPYROS

The women are now the executive branch?

CHREMES

                      Correct.

BLEPYROS

And all our civic duties. . . ?

CHREMES

                  . . . are women's work.

BLEPYROS

So court is not my job any more—it's my wife's?

CHREMES

Support is not your job any more—it's your wife's.

BLEPYROS

No more groaning myself awake at sunup?

CHREMES

No more. From this day forward, leave that to the girls.
Roll over in bed and exchange your groans for blissful
farts.

BLEPYROS

    This could turn nasty. We're not as young
as we were, and with women in the driver's seat . . . Suppose
they put the pressure on and coerce us . . .

CHREMES

Into what?

BLEPYROS

Coerce us into coition.

CHREMES

Screw *them*.

BLEPYROS

That's just
what I mean.

CHREMES

But what if we can't?

BLEPYROS

I suppose they'll cut off
our food. We'll die.

CHREMES

Then screw away for dear life.

BLEPYROS

Coition upon coercion. Degrading prospect.

CHREMES

Be firm. A man should be able to stand up under
any disaster for his country's good: An ancient
tradition declares that every idiot blunder
we pass into law will sooner or later redound
to Athens' profit.
                    —O Queen Athene, O
—in fact—all other Members of the Pantheon, *please*
do let this rock redound in the proper fashion.
—I'm leaving. Goodbye, Blepyros.

BLEPYROS

Chremes, goodbye.

Chremes exits into House III, Blepyros into House I.
A pause, and the Chorus enters left. They
are still dressed as men.

FIRST KORYPHAIA

For-WARD, MARCH!

Did anyone notice a Man behind us?

SECOND KORYPHAIA

Rear-WARD, SEARCH! Secure yourselves; these narrow places
are the favorite haunts of the base, unprincipled, sharpeyed male.
So, guard your rear. If enemy eyes should pierce our disguises,
all I can say is that ours would be a sorry tale.

36

FIRST SEMICHORUS

Singing as they step forward firmly.

> March in a masculine manner,
> stride with a virile thud.
> If a wiggle or sashay
> gives our secret away,
> we'll be lost to honor,
> and our name'll be mud.

Singly as, their resolution breaking, they mill around.

> —So close your cloaks. —And don't leave gaps.
> —We can't afford the littlest lapse
> in our vigilance. —Look left. —Look right.
> —Both ways at once! —And keep wrapped up tight.
> —If our cover slips, our victory
> is canceled,—kaputt,—a catastrophe!

FIRST KORYPHAIA

Speaking, as she tries to rearrange them.

> All right, but let's get moving. We've nearly come back safe
> and dry to the start of our March on Congress—journey's end.
> Look, there's the house of our newly elected Commander-in-Chief,
> the girl who conceived the scheme that is now the Law of the Land.

SECOND SEMICHORUS

Singing as they step off firmly again.

> Press on ahead—don't loiter,
> don't lag along in your beard.
> If we're recognized this way
> in the hard light of day,
> our images will shatter
> and our pitch'll be queered.

Singly as they mill around in panic.

> —I can't go on in this disguise.
> I'm changing. —But where? The walls have eyes.
> —Well, this wall doesn't. —Where? —Over here.
> —Someone keep a lookout. —I'm shedding this gear.
> —A man any more I refuse to be.
> —Oh, where is the girl I used to be?

*The Chorus members cluster by House III and
shed their disguises; their leaders try to maintain
some order. The Second Koryphaia looks off left.*

SECOND KORYPHAIA

> All right, but don't drag it out so. Look, here comes our Commander
> back from Congress, and she and her friends are already dressed
> like women again. Don't greet her half-changed; it might offend her.
> And strip your jaws of those awful beards, and strip them fast.

The Chorus is still completing its transformation
as Praxagora enters left, followed by the First,
Second, and Third Women. They carry
their male paraphernalia.

PRAXAGORA

Well, ladies, luck has been in attendance upon us;
our venture has fully attained its projected goals.

Sliding into paratragedy.

> *But speed is needed, lest some man perceive:*
> *Doff me your weeds, come bid the lowly clog*
> *Go footless off, let slack the knotted nodules*
> *Of Spartan harness . . .*

THIRD WOMAN

What'd she say?

FIRST WOMAN

Untie
your shoes.

PRAXAGORA

And chuck those canes.

To the First Koryphaia.

Look here, would you
get them fixed up in something like order? I'd like
to slip inside before my husband sees me
and put his cloak back where I got it—to say
nothing of all this other stuff I took.

FIRST KORYPHAIA

With a wave at the Chorus.

We've carried out all your orders already, and now we need your
advice; we long to be briefed: Just what do we do for a sequel?
You command our complete compliance in any suggested
    procedure;
for all-round feminine know-how, I never have seen your equal.

PRAXAGORA

Then wait right here. Be back in a minute to make you privy
to all the problems of this great office to which I'm elected.
You stood shoulder to shoulder with me when the going was heavy;
I'll need your masculine prowess to get my programs effected.

Gear in hand, she starts to enter House I, but is
greeted by the emerging Blepyros, who
is still in her clothes.

BLEPYROS

Well, well. Praxagora. Where've you been?

PRAXAGORA

                                    What business
is that of yours, sir?

BLEPYROS

                   What business of mine? Now, *there's*
aplomb.

PRAXAGORA
        Oh, come. You can't be implying that I've
been sleeping around with anyone.

BLEPYROS

                                    Any one, no.
Any two, any five, any twenty, perhaps.

PRAXAGORA

                                    Still no.
My purity's open to proof. Proceed.

BLEPYROS

                        Well, how?

PRAXAGORA
A simple sniff of my earlobes.

He complies dubiously.

                        Well?

BLEPYROS

                        Well, what?

PRAXAGORA
Well, any perfume?

BLEPYROS

                Why, no.

PRAXAGORA

                        You see? I'm pure.

BLEPYROS
A woman can't be banged with deodorized lobes?

PRAXAGORA
This woman can't.

BLEPYROS

                   All right, then: Why *did* you snaffle
my cloak and sneak out so early?

PRAXAGORA

                                       I was sitting up
with a pregnant friend.
                       She sent for me late last night
when her labor started.

BLEPYROS

                     You might have stopped to explain.

PRAXAGORA

Can you delay a delivery? I had to hurry.

BLEPYROS

Without one word? There's something suspicious here.

PRAXAGORA

Oh no, there isn't. I went as I was. The woman
who came was very insistent.

BLEPYROS

                         Did she insist
that you take my cloak? That you strip your husband's body
and flick this filmy thing on him, and leave him there,
laid out like a corpse? All I needed was a wreath
and a bottle of ritual oil.

PRAXAGORA

                      It was cold out, darling.
I wrapped poor little, delicate me in this cloak
to keep warm . . . as warm as you were, cuddled snug
in all those covers. That's the way I left you.

BLEPYROS

And that's the way my slippers left me, too,
and my cane hobbled off. Just what was the object of *that*?

PRAXAGORA

To ward off robbers. I switched our shoes, and clumped
along flatfooted, just like you, and banged
the cane on the pavement, to throw up a curtain of noise.
It saved you your cloak.

BLEPYROS

                     And lost us eight quarts of wheat—
I couldn't go down to Congress to draw my pay.

PRAXAGORA

Don't worry; nothing miscarried.

BLEPYROS

                         At Congress?

PRAXAGORA

                                        Er—no;
my friend—a lovely boy.
                    Did Congress meet?

BLEPYROS
You knew damned well it was meeting. I told you last night.

PRAXAGORA
Of course you did. I'd forgotten.

BLEPYROS
                        You haven't heard
the latest decree?

PRAXAGORA
                Why, no. Not at all. Not me.

BLEPYROS
Then sit right down in clover and take your ease.
By congressional action, the city is now in the hands
of you women.

PRAXAGORA
                And what do we do with it? Darn it?

BLEPYROS
                                        Dammit,
no. You govern.

PRAXAGORA
                What do we govern?

BLEPYROS
                            You govern
the government. The entire structure of Athenian society.

*Chremes emerges from House III and
listens unnoticed.*

PRAXAGORA
Aphrodite be blessed, but this is a happy day!
What a Great Society* Athens is going to have!

BLEPYROS
Great? Why great?

PRAXAGORA
                Oh, oodles of reasons. First,
it freely extends to every soul in Athens
a deal that's new, a deal that's fair. The future
holds no place for the Operator's sly maneuvers:
No more false witness, no more informing . . .

BLEPYROS

                                                    No more
of this, for god's sake; you're taking away my living.

CHREMES

Crossing to Blepyros.

        Kindly shut up and allow your wife to continue.

PRAXAGORA

An end to theft, to keeping up with the neighbors;
an end to the poor, ill-clad, ill-housed, ill-fed;
an end to public slander; an end to foreclosures.

CHREMES

I swear that Great Society's going to be
the absolute end. Provided it all comes true.

PRAXAGORA

I'll demonstrate my programs, point by point. By the time
I'm done, you'll back me all the way, and he

Pointing at Blepyros.

        won't have a single argument left to rebut with.

CHORUS

Gathering around Praxagora to urge her on.

                      Now prod and chivvy
                      your prudent savvy.
            Awake your superhuman acumen.
                      Let mind and heart
                      take an equal part
    in defending the Day of the Common Woman.
                      Hone your intelligence;
                      help our citizens
    increase their status without dishonor.
                      Come, institute
                      the Welfare State
    and make Prosperity turn the corner.
                      It's time to try
                      some bold *trouvaille*;
    a startling stroke is needed, quick.
                      But don't essay
                      some stale cliché . . .
    the audience hates a worn-out *shtick*.

FIRST KORYPHAIA

So hurry and start up your plan. Remember the spectators'
    standards:
Better early than good, and better never than late.

PRAXAGORA

I'm perfectly sure the advice I have to impart is good, but
the audience makes me anxious; how broad are their minds? how
    modern?
Will they approve of progress, or insist on remaining mired
in extinct tradition?

CHREMES

With a wave which includes the audience.
                    Don't worry about us, ma'am. We're compulsive
progressives. There's only one tradition left in Athens:
The past is passé; suppress it.

PRAXAGORA

Stepping forward.
                            I humbly request your attention.
Do not interrupt the proposal, please, before you have heard it,
and kindly refrain from rebuttal until you have grasped the
    concept.*
—Compulsory Universal Community Property is what I propose
to propose; across-the-board Economic Equality, to fill
those fissures that scar our society's face. No more the division
between Rich and Poor; the gap that partitions the squire who lolls
at ease on his acres from the wretch who's pressed to locate a plot
to rot away his final rest in; the gulf that secludes the nabob,
swimming in slaves, from the needy nudnick who can't afford
a second-hand footman.
                    Such segregation must go!
                                        Instead,
I'll institute total communalization: We'll wear the same clothes,
and share the same food . . .

BLEPYROS

                    What sort of food will we share?

PRAXAGORA

Furious at the interruption.
                                        Oh, *shit!*

BLEPYROS

So? You can have my share.

PRAXAGORA

                    No, no, I didn't mean *that.*
AS I WAS ABOUT TO SAY WHEN I WAS SO RUDELY
    INTERRUPTED:
My initial move will be to communalize land, and money,
and all other property, personal and real. From the Common Fund

thus created, we women will then proceed to supply you, employing
our talents for Budgeting, Eking Out, and Thinking Ahead.

BLEPYROS

But take the landless man who's invisibly wealthy . . . because
he hides his silver and gold in his pockets. What about him?

PRAXAGORA

He'll deposit it all in the Fund.

BLEPYROS

                                Suppose he keeps it?

PRAXAGORA

                                                Well, then
he'll be guilty of perjury.

BLEPYROS

                          He's guilty already. That's how he got it.

PRAXAGORA

But keeping it simply won't do him any good.

BLEPYROS

                                          It won't?

PRAXAGORA

Economic motives, the pressures of want, will cease to exist
when everyone owns everything from bread to cake, from wine
to woolies, from filets to fillets. So where is the profit in *not*
depositing?
          Well?
                  If you find an answer, please expound.

BLEPYROS

Well, these men with money . . . they're all thieves.

PRAXAGORA

                                    They *were* . . .
during the obsolete system of the *ancien regime*. But now,
when all the needs and means of existence are common and open
to all, I repeat: Where is the possible profit in *not*
depositing?

BLEPYROS

                    Suppose he sees a pretty young piece and decides
to plunge a little. He'll need to dip into private capital
to entice the girl into bed before he puts in for a share
in her assets.

PRAXAGORA

Pointless. Your man will be able to sleep with her free.
I'm pooling the women, creating a public hoard for the use
of every man who wishes to take them to bed and make babies.

BLEPYROS

You'll start a war. The men will all be shoving to stick
the best-stacked girl in stock.

PRAXAGORA

They'll be arranged in rows,
the ugly and snub-nosed right beside the really divine.
The man who wants the latter will have to take a crack
at the gruesome first.

BLEPYROS

That's quite a layout. But have a heart
for us senior citizens. If we have to dicker with the real dogs first,
we won't have any cock left by the time we've screwed our way
to the raving beauties at the end of the queue.

PRAXAGORA

They won't complain.
Don't worry yourself about it. Cheer up. They won't complain.

BLEPYROS

About what?

PRAXAGORA

About not getting laid.

BLEPYROS

That's just what happens with
you.*
—From the women's angle, this seems a remarkable stop-gap
   measure.
There won't be an unplugged loophole left in town. But you haven't
gone to the root of the matter; the men may be left hanging.
The women'll shy away from the ugly ones, and spread
themselves on the handsome.

PRAXAGORA

The total losses will keep an eye
on the hero types as they leave dinner, and patrol them in public.
Then, too, we'll enjoin the women from climbing in bed with the
   swell
and the tall before they've raised the spirits and warmed the
   cockles
of the grisly and squat.

46

BLEPYROS

You mean the flattest nose in Athens*
can hold its head as high as any Adonis?

PRAXAGORA

The pure democratic
ideal. A perfect comedown to all those finicky, ring-fingered,
stuck-up dandies, when a clodhoppered slob can cut in and say,
"Observe the rules of order: As soon as my rider's enacted,
I'll yield her to you to second the motion."

BLEPYROS

A system like this
requires a pretty wise father to know his own children.

PRAXAGORA

But why does
he need to? Age is the new criterion: Children will henceforth
trace their descent from all men who *might* have begot them.

BLEPYROS

A mighty
strain on an overstrung family tie; it should dispose
of every old man in the city. Remember, parricide pays.
These days, at least, a son only strangles the father he *knows*.
But introduce doubt, and the kids will happily work down the list
and, freed from the finer filial feelings, cover their victims
with shit.

PRAXAGORA

Oh, no. The neighbors simply won't permit it.
The old-style laissez-faire father could afford to stand idly by
while the man next door was sapped by his son; he couldn't care less.
But the new, collective father knows, when he hears a howl
of parental pain, that *he* is involved. If he doesn't stop
the slaughter, the boys might get him next.

BLEPYROS

You do have a point.
But I'd be appalled to hear the greeting "Poppa!" slip
from the lips of some of the young punks here—Epikouros, say,
or Leukólophos.

CHREMES

Looks like a worse disaster could happen.

BLEPYROS

Such as?

CHREMES

If that slimy pervert Aristyllos decided that you were his daddy,
and kissed you full on the mouth.

BLEPYROS

                          Coming from him, that's rape.
I'd make him yell to high heaven.

CHREMES

                      It's also halitosis, friend;
he'd make you smell like hell.

PRAXAGORA

                    No fear of a kiss like that:
Aristyllos was born before the act was passed.

BLEPYROS

                                Saved.

But that was a mighty near thing.
                    —Who's going to work the land
and produce the food?

PRAXAGORA

                The slaves. This leaves you just one civic
function: When the shades of night draw on, slip sleekly down
to dinner.

BLEPYROS

        That doesn't dispose of the question of clothes, the source
of supply for cloaks.

PRAXAGORA

                The ones you're wearing should last at first;
and then we'll weave you new ones.

BLEPYROS

                But a man who loses a suit
in court—where does he find the funds to discharge the judgment?
It wouldn't be right to tap the public till.

PRAXAGORA

                    To begin with,
the action at law is a thing of the past. No suits.

CHREMES

To Blepyros.

                      Now, *that*
is a sentence that spells the end of your existence.*

BLEPYROS

                          Precisely

what I was thinking.

PRAXAGORA
      What reason would there be for lawsuits?

BLEPYROS
A raft of reasons. To take just one, let's say a debtor
refuses to pay.

PRAXAGORA
     But where did the creditor get the money
to lend? All funds are public; he's ipso facto a thief.

CHREMES
Now, *there* is a lovely piece of deduction.

BLEPYROS
        Well, let her deduce me
this one: A communal dinner leads to a mugging. How, pray,
do the guilty parties pay the fine for drunken assault?
I think I've got you stumped.

PRAXAGORA
       We'll garnishee the hoodlum's rations
and stamp out that saucy behavior. The way to a man's deportment
is through his stomach.

BLEPYROS
       You mean there won't be an honest-to-
 goodness
robber remaining in town?

PRAXAGORA
      How can you rob yourself?

BLEPYROS
And no more thugs to steal your clothes when they meet you at
 night?

CHREMES
Try sleeping at home; you'll be safe.

PRAXAGORA
        No need to change your habits.
Sleep wherever you wish. You'll still be safe. Life's little
necessities will be provided for all. If someone starts
to strip you, give him your clothes as a present; don't kick up a
 feckless
fuss. There are better clothes for the taking to all who will toddle
down to the public storehouse.

BLEPYROS
      But certainly men will still gamble—
a friendly roll of the cubes?

PRAXAGORA

                      With nothing to feed the poor kitty?

BLEPYROS

What sort of society do you intend to establish?

PRAXAGORA

                            Communal.
Share and share alike. I'll knock out walls and remodel
the City into one big happy household, where all can come
and go as they choose.

BLEPYROS

            And where will you locate the dining room?

PRAXAGORA

I'm converting all the lawcourts. Justice must be served.

BLEPYROS

Then what becomes of the dock?

PRAXAGORA

                 I'm stocking the dock with crocks
of wine and flasks of water, and packing the bench with relays
of boys to provide entertainment—hymns to our wartime heroes,
interspersed with lampoons on slackers. Enough to shame the
    cowards
away from the dinner table.

BLEPYROS

               By Apollo, that sounds attractive.
But what becomes of the urns we used for choosing the juries?*

PRAXAGORA

I'll set them up in the market, and form the citizens in lines
by Harmodios' statue. Each one in turn will draw from the urn
a letter that shows his assignment.

BLEPYROS

                   Assignment to court?

PRAXAGORA

                             No, lunch.
Each eating place will bear a different letter. Therefore,
the man who draws Kappa will eat in the Kourt of Klaims; Epsilon,
Equity; Delta, Divorce.

BLEPYROS

            And Beta?

PRAXAGORA

                               Probate.

BLEPYROS

                                          But what

about Pi?

PRAXAGORA

        We'll let him eat cake in Appeal.

BLEPYROS

                                   And where does this

leave Eta?

PRAXAGORA

           He's already eaten.

BLEPYROS

                        But the poor unlettered chap

who draws a blank—the rest will drive him away from the table?

PRAXAGORA

           I rather think you misunderstand.
           The State's not going to stint. Its hand
           is full and open, its heart is large,
           it'll stuff its menfolk free of charge,
           then issue them torches when dinner's done
           and send them out to hunt for fun.

FIRST WOMAN*

           And fun they'll find, in alleys crowded
           with women panting, "How's about it?"
           with women rustling at their heels
           and spinning their heads with sexy spiels:
           "Come change your luck. I happen to know
           a hot little nymphet who's ready to go."

SECOND WOMAN

           Then another one shouts, from a window above,
           "Why not try a higher type of love?
           The girl up here is an absolute dream,
           stacked like a statue, peaches and cream. . . ."

BLEPYROS

Imitating an old woman.

           "There's just one thing; before she's free,
           you'll have to try a fall with me."

PRAXAGORA

> But that's for the dandies, the gay young blades.
> Priority rating for pretty maids
> goes to the uglies, the awkward crew . . .
> goes, in short, to men like you.
> So when you see some passionate sprout
> go sprinting past you, set up a shout:

THIRD WOMAN

Imitating an old man.

> "Hey, where's the fire? What makes you run?
> Getting there is all the fun
> you're going to have. Just read the decree:
> Revolting, disgusting types like me
> take pride of place in these affairs. . . ."

BLEPYROS

Caught up in the possibilities.

> "But if you want, you can wait downstairs
> and pass the time while I'm inside
> with a little friction, self-applied."

PRAXAGORA

Well, I trust this satisfies you both.

BLEPYROS & CHREMES

> And how.

PRAXAGORA

I'd better be going downtown. Since they elected
me C-in-C, there's so much to *do*. Provide
for receipt of that incoming cash. Procure a girl
with a nice shrill voice to handle public announcements.
And that's not all. I've got to arrange for the dinner.
Your first communal banquet's tonight.

BLEPYROS

> So soon?

PRAXAGORA

You have my word. And then I propose to stamp out
prostitution. Every whore will be forced to shut up
shop.

BLEPYROS

A broad proposal. But why?

PRAXAGORA

> It's perfectly

plain.

Indicating the Chorus.

> Consider these ladies here.

BLEPYROS

                                 They're perfectly
plain.

PRAXAGORA

             Exactly. If whores are left in business,
these ladies won't get a chance at the handsome boys.
I shall also put an end to depilatory practices
by female slaves, a most underhanded ploy
they employ for snatching lovers away from their mistresses.
Henceforth, they're back at scratch, and will choose their bedmates
to fit their proper bracket. Free love should be
for the free.

BLEPYROS

As Praxagora makes to go.

                      I think I'll follow along with you
and stick by your side. I can feel those admiring glances,
hear those envious whispers: "There goes our Commander's
husband, the man behind a successful woman."

CHREMES

And I'm supposed to deposit my goods and chattels
downtown. But I'd better take stock of my property first.

Chremes enters House III. Praxagora, Blepyros,
*and the First, Second, and Third Women exit right.**

CHORAL INTERLUDE*

  .   .   .   .

Chremes, deep in thought, emerges from House III.
During the succeeding sequence, servants keep
coming from the house at his direction, bearing
kitchen utensils which they arrange before him
rather in the fashion of a festival parade.

CHREMES

I love to parade my wares, and such a solemn
occasion calls for a holy procession. But who's
to lead it?
           Of course.
                   —Dear sister sifter,* hither;
you're to be Queen. (No one's holier than she is.)
Proceed in powdered purity, impeccable product
of bushels of grain. You will refine the whole
procession with your presence. But who will bear your litter?
—Trashbucket outside!
                 You're looking a little pale;

your inside's black, in fact. You might have been dyeing
Lysikrates' beard.

       —Now for a lady-in-waiting.
Waterclock, hurry out here—you've got the time.
—And then someone to carry the ritual pitcher.
That's a tough one . . .

         Pitcher, get out here!

             Contain
yourself, and you may make quite a splash.

             —Strike up
the band!

A chamber pot is brought on.

      You'll get them moving, the way you do me
in the morning, running the gamut from tinkles to roars.
—A coffer for offerings; a cruet to bear the olive;
two tripods to lend some status.

           —Who'll carry the banner?
The flagon.

      —And now release the weaker vessels
to bring up the rear.

         But mind you, ladles first.

He surveys the procession happily. Pheidolos,
fuming, bursts out of House II.

PHEIDOLOS

Turn in what belongs to me! That'll be the day.
I'll have to be pretty badly off, without
a brain in my head to call my own.

          Dammit,
I'll never do it!

      Or first I'll inspect this business
from top to bottom, and see what I can find out.
I've led a thrifty, hardworking life; I refuse
to wash my hands of all that honest sweat
for no good reason. This whole affair needs plumbing.

Seeing Chremes' procession.

     —What sort of crackpot setup is this? You moving?
Or proposing to hock these crocks?

CHREMES

         Not at all.

PHEIDOLOS

          Then why
the formation? A new line of pots for the auction block?

CHREMES
You don't understand. I'm making them over . . .

PHEIDOLOS
Taking
them in for repairs?

CHREMES
No, no. I'm making them over
to the City. I'm taking them down to the market and turning
them in. The law's in force.

PHEIDOLOS
You really intend
to turn them in?

CHREMES
I certainly do.

PHEIDOLOS
God save you,
you *are* a sap.

CHREMES
How so?

PHEIDOLOS
How so? It's simple.

CHREMES
You mean I shouldn't obey the Law?

PHEIDOLOS
You *do*
need help, boy. Law—what law?

CHREMES
The law that's in force.

PHEIDOLOS
The law that's in force. Of all the asinine statements.

CHREMES
Asinine?

PHEIDOLOS
What else? Of all the lackwitted lumps
on earth, you take the cake.

CHREMES
Because I do
what I'm told?

PHEIDOLOS
To do what you're told—is that the Way
of the Wise Man?

CHREMES
> Without a doubt.

PHEIDOLOS
> It's the Way of the Chump.

CHREMES
I gather you don't intend to deposit yours?

PHEIDOLOS
Well . . . holding off for a little. Waiting to see
the consensus.

CHREMES
> But *everyone's* ready to turn in his goods.
The only conceivable consensus.

PHEIDOLOS
> Seeing's believing;
I haven't seen a sign of it yet.

CHREMES
> They're saying it
on every street in the City.

PHEIDOLOS
> Say it, they would.

CHREMES
They pledge to deliver in person.

PHEIDOLOS
> Pledge it, they would.

CHREMES
Your irony's wearing me down.

PHEIDOLOS
> Iron it, they would.

CHREMES
May god please damn you to hell.

PHEIDOLOS
> Damn it, they would.
Can you believe that any Athenian capable
of connected thought will give his goods to the State?
It's not in our culture pattern: We, by god,
are a nation of Takers.
> And so, by god, are the Gods.
That's easily seen from their statues; look at the hands.
We pray for a gift from Heaven . . . but there they stand,
hands out, palms *up*. No, they're not planning to give;
they Take.

CHREMES

Sir, you amaze me. But let me get on
with my work. I have to get this packed. Now where
did I put that strap?

PHEIDOLOS

You're truly taking it in?

CHREMES

I swear I am. Watch closely: First, I tie
these tripods together . . .

PHEIDOLOS

But this is lunacy! Why
so hasty? Delay a little. See what action
others take. And then, at length, in the fullness
of time . . .

CHREMES

Do what?

PHEIDOLOS

Well, stall. Defer. And then
you might try Putting Off.

CHREMES

While waiting for what?

PHEIDOLOS

The earthquake, creep!

CHREMES

What earthquake?

PHEIDOLOS

Earthquakes happen.
Or lightning might strike. A polecat could cross your path:
an omen like that is bound to stop these deposits.

CHREMES

It might be a positive blessing if I couldn't find
room to make my deposit?

PHEIDOLOS

Room for a rebate,
you mean. But don't worry. Wait a day, even two . . .
you'll still have room for deposit.

CHREMES

What do you mean?

PHEIDOLOS

Pointing at the audience.

> I know this crew: The fastest voters in Greece . . .
> and equally quick to renege on whatever they vote.

CHREMES

Friend, they'll deliver.

PHEIDOLOS

> Supposing they don't turn it in?

CHREMES

Then we'll turn it in.

PHEIDOLOS

> Supposing they won't let you in?

CHREMES

We'll start a holy war.

PHEIDOLOS

> Supposing they win?

CHREMES

I'll chuck my stuff and run.

PHEIDOLOS

> Supposing they sell it?

CHREMES

Drop dead.

PHEIDOLOS

> Supposing I do drop dead?

CHREMES

> I suppose
> I'd be in your debt.

PHEIDOLOS

> You persist in this futile yearning
> to turn in your goods?

CHREMES

> I certainly do.

Pointing at the audience.

> Just look
> at my neighbors here; they're coming across.

PHEIDOLOS

> Oh, sure.
> Take Antisthenes there, the well-known theatrical man—
> I can see *him* producing. He'd rather do something
> tasteful—like sitting on the pot for a month-long run.

CHREMES
Damn *you*.

PHEIDOLOS
   Or Kallimachos there, the well-known director:
How much can he manage?

CHREMES
       More than Kallias can—
the well-known bankrupt.

PHEIDOLOS
     Whatever Kallias has,
he'll waste it himself. He doesn't need help from the city.

CHREMES
All these gibes at our laws—they're hardly fair.

PHEIDOLOS
So what's to be fair? Should I pretend I'm blind,
and haven't seen the dissolving decrees our Congress
turns out? Recall that triumph of planned economy—
the ceiling on salt?*

CHREMES
     Well, salt *was* pretty expensive.

PHEIDOLOS
And where is it now?

CHREMES
     Well, salt is right out of sight.

PHEIDOLOS
I suppose you've forgotten the copper coinage we voted
when silver was short?*

CHREMES
     It caught me shorter. I can't
remember a baser issue. My mouth was stuffed
with the coppers I got for my grapes, and over I went
to the market to use them to buy some barley. And just
as I was holding out my sack to be filled,
the crier cut loose:
    "WE'RE OFF THE COPPER STANDARD.
ONLY SILVER IS LEGAL TENDER, EFFECTIVE
NOW!"
  It still brings a lump to my throat.

PHEIDOLOS

But don't
neglect our latest winner, that direct assessment
of two-and-a-half percent that was certain to yield
the City forty talents clear. You know,
Euripides' bill.*
And everyone gilded Euripides'
lily . . . until it developed the bill was the usual
blather, and nobody paid, and the mudslinging started . . .
and our guilty Golden Boy turned out to be Tar-Baby.

CHREMES

But all that happened when *we* were in charge. Now things
have changed. The women have taken control.

PHEIDOLOS

And I'll
take care. They may have taken the throne, but they won't
piss on me just to hear it splash.

CHREMES

Now, what does
that gibberish mean?

To House III.
—Hey, boy, bring out the yoke!
A servant obeys, and Chremes continues his packing.
Shortly, Praxagora's newly appointed Town Crieress,
a girl with a very shrill voice, enters right.

CRIERESS

CITIZENS ALL: If you're male, adult, and Athenian,
a word for YOU from our new Commistress-in-Chief:
The word is FOOD!
And it's FREE!
So beat the crowds
downtown and draw for seats! But wherever you sit,
there's PLENTY FOR ALL:
Tables loaded bowlegged
beneath a Complete Selection of Gourmet Goodies!
Luxurious *Couches* smothered in Pillows to ease
the Discriminating Diner! A corps of Winsome *Waitresses*!*
Ready-Blended *Wines* by the bowlful! And FOOD?
There's lots and it's hot: Those tasty *Filets,* that spicy
barbecued *Rabbit,* those bursting-with-goodness *Cakes,*
those crunchy *Sweetmeats* to fill in the chinks . . . PLUS
Party *Garlands* for ALL! AND ALL TOPPED OFF

with a bubbling *Broth* whipped up by charming cookettes
in their very own pipkins!

      (All items are tested
by our taster Smoios, who subjects each dish that comes in
to the rigorous probe of his educated tongue. He keeps
the girls in the kitchen right on their toes, I tell you.)

THIS IS A MENU FOR YOU MEN! And age is no object:
The saddest gaffer shucks off his rags and clogs,
and slips on a spruce wool cloak and sumptuous shoes,
as young in heart as the lad who laughs beside him.
SO HURRY! RUSH! The rolls are now being served;
an open mouth at the door ensures satisfaction!

She exits right. A pause.

PHEIDOLOS
I might as well mosey on over. No point in staying
here. After all, it's the will of the City.

CHREMES
        You haven't
turned in your property. Where do you think you're going?

PHEIDOLOS
To dinner.

CHREMES
     Oh, no. If those women have any sense,
you'll have to make your deposit first.

PHEIDOLOS
         I'll make it.

CHREMES
But when?

PHEIDOLOS
     I'm hardly the man to keep my Nation
waiting.

CHREMES
     Meaning?

PHEIDOLOS
      That others are bound to turn
their stuff in later than I do.

CHREMES
       And so you'll mosey
on over to dinner regardless?

PHEIDOLOS

I have no choice:
At times like these, the truly patriotic man
obliterates his own desires, and does what he can
to aid the State.

CHREMES

Supposing they won't let you in?

PHEIDOLOS
I'll butt my way in.

CHREMES

Supposing they beat you up?

PHEIDOLOS
I swear I'll sue.

CHREMES

Supposing they laugh in your face?

PHEIDOLOS
I'll take a firm stand.

CHREMES

On what?

PHEIDOLOS

On the stoop, and grab
the food as they carry it in.

CHREMES

Then go if you must,
but let me get there first.
To House III.

—Sikon, Parmenon,
come get this moving. That's the lot.
Two servants emerge and gather up the utensils.
Chremes leads them off to the right.

PHEIDOLOS

Well, look,
I'll help you carry it . . .

CHREMES

Not on your life, you won't.
I'm not going to hand this over to our Commistress
only to have you claim it belongs to you.
Exeunt, right, Chremes, his servants, and his
receptacles—with the exception of the chamber pot,
which lies forgotten before his house.

PHEIDOLOS

Oh lord, I need a genuinely subtle gimmick
to wangle a place with those clowns at the public trough
without giving up what's mine.

Now, what?*

His eye lights on the chamber pot.

Of course!

I see it all.

He grabs up the pot.

But I'd better dash. I'll have to
go in to dinner when they do. No time to waste.

Clutching Chremes' chamber pot, he races off right.

CHORAL INTERLUDE

· · · · · · · · ·

*House II is now the home of a Hag, who appears
on the roof and tries, with no success, to
assume an alluring posture. She may be succinctly
described as the third ugliest woman in the world.*

HAG

Why don't the Men get here? They're way overdue.
And here I am, ready and waiting, with all this beauty
going to waste. My complexion's slathered with pancake,
my figure's trim and firm in my best yellow shrug,
I'm humming a song in my heart . . .

but it's not for real.

It needs a *Man*. And so do I—a Man
to snag as he goes by here.

—O Muses, descend

right into my mouth. Bring along an Ionian song . . .
pretty, and not too loud, but pretty lewd.

*A Sweet Young Thing appears on the roof of
House III. Her prettiness matches the ugliness
of the Hag, whom she addresses.*

SWEET YOUNG THING

Oh, look; Dry Rot's set in. My, aren't we up early?
You thought you'd slip in and poach a little while I
was out; inveigle some poor egg upstairs
with your singing. All right, then, sing—and I'll come on
with a song in rebuttal.

Aside.

—I know this antiphonal bit
is liable to bore the audience stiff, but it's really
pleasant enough. No comedy should be without it.

HAG

*Showing a large leather phallos.**

> Here's a friend, little girl; run off and play
> with yourself.

> —MUSIC!

A fluteplayer appears.

> Vamp an accompaniment, honey;
> blow me a tune that does us both some credit.

She sings to the flute's accompaniment.

> If pleasure's your aim, drop into my bed,
>   where satisfaction is guaranteed.
> Don't try it with girls—they're limited;
>   a Woman responds to your every need.
> Girls are stiff, and they cool down fast;
>   girls run off when other men call.
> But Women smolder, and women last:
>   Maturity makes it; ripeness is all.

SWEET YOUNG THING

Singing.

> You can't fight nature; don't criticize
> the girls. True sensuous feminine bliss
> buds on their breasts and blooms in their thighs,
> while you spread powder and paint by the pot
> to putty time's craters, and make you the kiss
> of death. Confess it; Ripeness is rot.

HAG

Singing to the same tune.

> I wish you some very unnatural shocks
> when you lie fallow and itch to be plowed:
> I wish you a suddenly vanishing box,
> a suddenly crumbling bed to match,
> and the clammy touch, all curled and cowed,
> of a snake who never comes up to scratch.

The tune changes.

SWEET YOUNG THING

> What shall I do for pleasures?
>   My lover hasn't come.
> I'm left to my own resources,
>   and Mother isn't home . . .

*She breaks off the song and looks around indignantly,
as if for someone connected with the
production of the play. She speaks.*

> —I'm certainly not supposed to deliver the rest of this?

An obdurate silence. She shrugs resignedly and
returns to the song.

> So Granny, please, a favor:
> Bring up that great reliever,
> the lonely woman's savior
> and send it right on over
> to maneuver
> with me.

HAG

Holding the leather phallos, she sings
to the same tune.⁎

> You've caught the fatal itching
> (your lover hasn't come),
> that decadent Eastern letching
> (your mother isn't home) . . .

Speaking.

> —There pants a girl who's ready to put the L in Lesbos.⁎

Returning to the song, she clutches the
phallos defensively.

> You can't abduct my lover,
> my clever little shaver . . .

SWEET YOUNG THING

> I'm beautiful as ever,
> and that's what you can never
> take over
> from me.

The music ends.

HAG

Sing all you want. Keep popping in and out
like a weasel in rut. You can't attract a man
before he drops in on *me*.

SWEET YOUNG THING

> To pay his last

respects?
> Confess it, crowbait, that was a new one.

HAG

Oh no, it wasn't.

SWEET YOUNG THING

> Why waste new jokes on a worn old

bag like you?

HAG

> My age won't bother you a bit.

SWEET YOUNG THING
What will? That slobbered rouge? That plaster that's plugging
the cracks?

HAG
This idle chatter is perfectly pointless.

SWEET YOUNG THING
Your presence is perfectly pointless. Why are you perching
there—what's up?

HAG
Just humming a song for Epígenês—
he's my young man.

SWEET YOUNG THING
I thought your only man
was eaten by moths years back.*

HAG
Just wait. You'll see;
my boy'll be here in a bit.
Looking off right.
And here he comes now.

SWEET YOUNG THING
For you? Oh, no. Whatever he needs, it's not
a case of plague.

HAG
I'm just what he lacks.

SWEET YOUNG THING
Like hemlock.
But let him tell you himself. I'm leaving.

HAG
Me, too.
You'll see that I know what I'm doing. Better than you.
*They disappear into their houses. Epigenes
enters right, carrying a torch, still garlanded from
the banquet. He is very young, very drunk,
and very ithyphallic. He sings.*

EPIGENES
I want to make sweet music tonight,
 I want my baby in bed.
I don't want to hump some rickety lump
 or overage eyesore instead.
I'm Athenian, male, of age, and free;
I won't put up with sex by decree.

The shutter in House II's window opens, and
the Hag appears. She sings to the same tune,
unnoticed by Epigenes.

HAG

Your vapid lays are out of date;
    the state is calling the tune.
The will of the people chooses your mate;
    you'll hump by the numbers, and soon.
Laissez-faire sex is a losing cause;
    Democracy's only as good as its laws.

Speaking, aside.

I'll go and spy on every move he makes.
She disappears into the house again,
closing the shutter.

EPIGENES

I come here stinking drunk and stuffed with a standing
desire for a certain living doll. Dear Gods:
please let me get her alone.
The shutter of House III's upper window opens,
and the Sweet Young Thing appears.

SWEET YOUNG THING

                I've pulled the wig
over that damnable granny's eyes. She's gone;
she really thought I'd stay inside.
Seeing Epigenes, who is fidgeting
uncertainly before her door.

                        Well, look
at this—the very boy we were talking about.
The music starts again, and she sings her
*half of a rather vapid love duet.**

The one way to love
lies this way, my love,
so come this way to love,
    my dear.
With me, up above
in bed, my love,
you'll love away the night
    right here.

I throb with lust   when I see the twist
    and the curl of your well-groomed hair.
The oddest passion   pervades my person;
    my maidenhood's abraded by its wear

                            and

                         tear . . .

So give way to love,
and don't wait to love,
relieve the weight of love
up here.

The door to House II opens and the Hag emerges.
She watches unnoticed as Epigenes sings his half
of the duet . . . after he has eagerly tried the
door of House III and found it locked.

EPIGENES

There's no way to love;
it's this way, my love:
the way says nay to love,
my dear.
So open, my love,
the doorway hereof,
or I'll cave in and lie
right here.
Love's made me deranged,   my brain is unhinged,
I'm a certified quivering mass.
I'm rabid to rest   on your luscious bust,
and beat a crazy rhythm on your glor-
ious

ass . . .

So give way to love,
and don't wait to love,
relieve the weight of love
down here.

The Sweet Young Thing disappears from her window.
Epigenes waits, then knocks. No reply. Frustrated,
he tries another song.

No words of mine can ever express
the tense extent of my need.
So here's a prayer in my distress
to which I hope you'll take heed:
Please open the door
and give me a kiss.
You got me this way;
don't leave me like this.

He waits, then knocks again. Still no reply.
He tries another verse.

The Goddess of Love gave you her face;
you're a living beauty spot.
You sing like a Muse, you move like a Grace . . .
Darling, what chance have I got?

> Please open the door
> and give me a kiss.
> You got me this way;
> don't leave me like this.

He waits, then knocks as the Hag crosses quickly
to a point just behind him.

HAG

I hear you knocking. Looking for me?

EPIGENES

Turning violently.

> What gives
> you that idea . . . uh, sir or madam, as the case
> may be?

HAG

> You nearly broke down my door. The latch
> is flapping.

EPIGENES

> It wasn't me, lady, I'd die before
> I'd touch your latch.

HAG

> With that torch, you must be looking
> for somebody—who?

EPIGENES

> I'm, uh, trying to deliver a warrant.*

HAG

Pretty nice subpoena you've got. Perhaps
I can serve it for you?

EPIGENES

> I'll handle this myself.

HAG

I know the neighborhood. Lad like you needs help
in these parts.

EPIGENES

> I'd really prefer to pull this off
> alone.

HAG

> Oh, no. I insist. Forget your pride.
> Besides, you can help me with *my* case.

EPIGENES

> But, lady, you're not
> on the docket!

HAG

It's been a while.

EPIGENES

We've built up such

a backlog . . .

HAG

I see.

EPIGENES

. . . that we've had to defer all actions
of more than sixty years' standing till there's another
sitting. We're only opening cases where
the matter at hand is under twenty years old.
I suggest you file your affidavit . . .

HAG

Too tender.

EPIGENES

. . . and wait.

HAG

No, honey. That was the old procedure. Under
this new regime, you have to process our cases
first.

EPIGENES

Oh, no. I can pass my turn. It's like
the rules in craps.

HAG

Did you pass your turn at dinner?
Just can that crap and let's get rolling.

EPIGENES

I'm afraid
I don't understand.
Turning back to the door of House III.

Now, if you'll excuse me, I've got
some pressing business behind this door. I'll knock.

HAG

Grabbing him away and spinning him around.

Enter by the main door only. So bang away
on this.

EPIGENES

But that's a triumphal archway. How
would I know if I'd knocked or not?

72

HAG

> 'Fess up; you love me.

You're just surprised they let me out.

EPIGENES

> I am.

HAG

It's madness. My reputation's ruined. But I don't care.
So pucker up.

EPIGENES

> I'm paralyzed; my pucker's stuck.

And what about your lover?

HAG

> Lover?

EPIGENES

> The eminent artist.

HAG

What artist?

EPIGENES

> The still-life man.* The one who lays out
those tasteful arrangements of corpses. Once he catches
you out, you're dead.

Shooing her away.

> So quick, now. Back inside.

HAG

Balking.

I know what you're up to.

EPIGENES

> And I sure as hell
know what you're up to. And the answer, lady, is no.

HAG

And I sure as heaven got you in the draw. I refuse
to let you go.

EPIGENES

> You're out of your head, you relic!

HAG

Poor fevered lad. I'm putting you to bed.
My bed.

EPIGENES

As she drags him toward House II.

> A tip for the handyman: Why waste money
> on bucket hooks? Just take a little old lady
> (every home has one), let her down in the well
> by her ankles, and presto, up comes the bucket, gripped
> in a vice.

HAG

> Flattery gets you nowhere, sweetie.
> This way. Follow me.

EPIGENES

> Impossible. You haven't paid
> the tax.

HAG

> What tax?

EPIGENES

> The use tax.* On this transaction,
> one-fifth of one percent of my total value,
> or else I don't come across.

HAG

> There's no withholding,
> even on a joint return. You'll do your duty
> free. A boy your age goes right to my head.

EPIGENES

> And a hag your age goes right to my stomach. You'll never
> get my consent.

HAG

Producing a scroll.

> Here's something to make you say yes.

EPIGENES

> What's that?

HAG

> A Law, the long and short of which is
> that you come along to my place pretty shortly.

EPIGENES

> No digests; read me the details.

HAG

> Delighted to do so:

Unrolling the scroll, she reads.

> *Be it decreed, by the Women sitting in Congress:*
> *As Sex is a National Resource, all private parts*
> *are hereby declared to be public. Free fornication*

between adolescents may take place only after
the male adolescent has first applied his resources
to the full satisfaction of a bonafide senile female.
But should said male refuse to fulfill these conditions
and yet persist in attempting to mate with an agemate,
said senile female may then, without let or hindrance,
proceed to take the part of said male—
                              and pull
as hard as she can until he agrees to give in.

EPIGENES
Talk about stretching the law. That's hitting below
the belt.*

HAG
                    Still, better obey it. In part and in whole.

EPIGENES
Can't one of my friends or neighbors go bail for me?
My credit's good.

HAG
                         Credit's abolished. No man
is good for more than he can raise on the spot.*

EPIGENES
I'll claim an exemption. I'll swear I'm unfit.

HAG
                                        You can't
wriggle out of this one.

EPIGENES
                         I'll plead the pressures of commerce:
This might disturb my business.

HAG
                              I couldn't care less
if your business drops off completely. You're caught.

EPIGENES
                                        Then what
do I do?

HAG
              You come along with me. This way.

EPIGENES
Is there no way out?

HAG
                    The way out and the way in
are one and the same.*

EPIGENES

Then make your bed ready first:
Strew it with plumes and broken blossoms, drape it
with crepe, bind up your head with fillets, place
the oil before the couch, and set the lustral
jug at the door.

And call the mourners.

HAG

You wait.
There's life in the old girl yet. You'll buy me a wreath
when I'm done with you.

EPIGENES

Don't doubt it. One made of wax—
black wax.* You're liable to fall apart before
you make it inside.

As they near House II, the Sweet Young Thing
appears at the door of House III.

SWEET YOUNG THING

Where are you dragging that man?

HAG

I'm taking him home.

SWEET YOUNG THING

Crossing to them.

You sleep with that slip of a lad?
I've heard of mother-love, but this is insane.
You can't be serious. He'd get lost. This law
will give our country an Oedipus complex.* Incest
is now the national family sport.

She pries the Hag loose from Epigenes
and pushes her away.

HAG

Just jealous,
that's you, you all-purpose slut. You won't get away
with this.

Shaking her fist, she exits into House II.
Epigenes turns to the Sweet Young Thing.

EPIGENES

O god, I'm saved, pulled back from the pit
in the nick of time. My darling, I swell with gratitude;
how can I ever repay you? Tonight I'll go down
on my knees before you and try to discharge my debt.

They start for House III. The door to House II
opens and discloses a Crone—the second ugliest
woman in the world. She scuttles across, grabs
Epigenes, and addresses the Sweet Young Thing.

CRONE

Hey, girlie, where do you think you're taking this?
Trying for a little bedtime tort, you tart?
Stick to the letter of the law: I get first dibs.

EPIGENES

I'm sunk again.

          And where did they dig you up,

you vision of decay?

              —The first was gruesome enough,

but this is catastrophe.

CRONE

              This way, pretty boy. March!

She drags him off toward House II, foiling
efforts by the Sweet Young Thing to save him.
Sadly, the Sweet Young Thing exits into House III.
Epigenes stretches yearningly after her as
the door closes.

EPIGENES

Darling! Don't desert me. Please don't allow
this scarecrow to take me in tow.

CRONE

              It's not me, honey.
You've been hooked by the long long arm of the Law.

EPIGENES

By the long long arm of the Goddess of Acne, all ready
to erupt.

CRONE

         Now be a good boy and come along nice.
No time for talking.

EPIGENES

           Well, first please let me sneak off
to the outhouse and try to recoup my courage, or else
you'll see a yellow streak spread right up my back.

CRONE

Buck up, ducky, and march. I've got a pot
up there. It's perfectly adequate.

EPIGENES
>Not for a man
who's scared as shitless as I'll be.
>>Can't two neighbors
bail me out of this mess? They'll put down a hefty
deposit.

CRONE
>You'll make your own deposit. Inside.

The door to House III opens, disclosing, not
the Sweet Young Thing, but a Harridan—
without doubt, the ugliest woman in the world.
She crosses and grabs Epigenes from behind.
He does not turn.

HARRIDAN
And where do you think you're jaunting off to with her?

EPIGENES
Believe me, this is no jaunt. It's more of a drag.

The Harridan pulls him loose from the Crone's
grasp. He still does not turn.

>No matter. A million thanks to you, whoever
you are. You've saved me from a fate that's literally
worse than . . .

He turns.

>Holy Herakles!
>>Pan the Paranoid!
Minions of madness!
>Kastor!
>>Pollux!
>>>*Help!*

Looking from the Crone to the Harridan.
>If that one's catastrophe, this is the end of the world.

To the audience.
>—Gentlemen, please, a suggestion:
>>What IS this thing?
A freshly painted baboon just back from a nose job?
An excavated ancestor, up from twenty years
in the cold cold ground?
>>Or what the hell?

HARRIDAN
Pulling him toward House III.
Flattery gets you nowhere, sweetie. This way.

CRONE
Pulling him toward House II.
>You mean *this* way.

HARRIDAN
                            Don't worry, darling. I'll never
let you go.

CRONE
           And neither, lovey, will I.

EPIGENES
Well, somebody better; this is vivisection. Go back
to hell, the both of you!

CRONE
                 As per the law,
you're coming along with me.

HARRIDAN
                    Not if a more
revolting old bag turns up.
                   And here I am!

EPIGENES
Please stop this tugging. If you two ruin me first,
what sort of shape will I be in to see my girl?

HARRIDAN
Well, that's your worry. Right now, you stick to business.

They pull harder.

EPIGENES
I'll stick, I'll stick.
               In order to win my freedom
I take on one of you. Which one?

HARRIDAN
                 No problem.
This way. March!

EPIGENES
Indicating the Crone.
            As soon as *she* lets go.

CRONE
You come along with me.

EPIGENES
Indicating the Harridan.
               If *she* lets go.

HARRIDAN
I'll never let you go.

CRONE
           And neither will I.

EPIGENES
Please, ladies, never go into the ferryboat business.

CRONE
Why not?

EPIGENES
You'll set your clients ashore on both banks
at once.

HARRIDAN
Shut up. By the left flank . . .

CRONE
Nope. By the right flank.

*The tug-of-war continues, but the advantage is to
the Harridan, and the group is moving
left, toward House III.*

EPIGENES
But this is double jeopardy. I'm standing the same charge
twice. That's half of me for each. Now, how
do I scull two leaky shells with a single oar?

HARRIDAN
A nice aphrodisiac diet does it, dearie:
a bag of truffles, a peck of onions, then back
to the sack.

EPIGENES
I'm just about at the end of my rope.
One step more to the door.

*The struggling party reaches House III, and
the Crone suddenly relaxes her grip.
She addresses the Harridan.*

CRONE
Don't think this means
you win; I'm dropping up to share the wealth.
Three can play at this game.

EPIGENES
They've raised the ante
by another granny. And *one* is too much for me.

HARRIDAN
Sonny, whoever told you you had a choice?

EPIGENES
Despairingly, to the audience.
I'd like to complain to Fate:
This is rather too much.
A night and a day of solid humping away

81

Indicating Harridan.
             on this female compost-heap entitles me
Indicating Crone.
                 to proceed to the bumpy embrace of this study in toadskin
                 and kiss the worst malocclusion in Greece.
                                              Unlucky
                 isn't the word; I am Cataclysmatically Doomed.
                 O Zeus the Savior, do what you can for a seaman
                 who's due to cast off soon with a monster cast.
                 And if worst comes to worst (and I've got both),
                 and my frail frigate sags beneath the weight
                 of a couple of slags like these and goes down with all hands,
                 then lay my battered body to rest at the inlet's
                 outlet, and mark the spot with a monument. Not
                 the usual funerary urn, however, nor
                 the sailor's solitary oar. Instead, a whore:
Indicating Harridan.
                 Take this old bitch, preserve her in pitch, and sink
                 her feet in lead right up to the ankles; then set
                 her over the grave of one who strove in the breach
                 but went down manfully, lost while crossing the gulf.
The Harridan and the Crone
drag him into House III.

        CHORAL INTERLUDE*
             .   .   .   .

The Crieress* staggers on, very drunk. She
has trouble keeping to the point.

        CRIERESS
        O happy people.
                      O gladsome native land.
        O blissfullest mistress mine.
                               O all you elated
        ladies clustered on your stoops.
                                  O merry men.
        O radiant neighbors.
                      O titillated townsfolk.
                                        Not
        to mention, O Me. I may be merely a menial,
        but god, do I smell nice. My head is drenched
        in the most expensive scents. But perfume pales
        before the scent of wine. Especially wine
        from Thasos. Comes in little bitty jugs,
        and goes to your head. The smell that tells. The spoor
        that endures. When other odors have flown. (Oh, god.)

So ask for the best. And mix it straight. And breathe
the night away in the blissful bouquet of bottled
beatitude!
                    —Oops. Where was I?

To the Chorus.

                                        —Ladies, where
can I find my mister?
                    I mean, of course, my mastress's
husband.

FIRST KORYPHAIA
                    Wait here. I think he'll come to you.

CRIERESS
Excellent.

Blepyros enters from House I with a
dancing girl on each arm.

                    And here he comes. He's on his way
to dinner.
                    —O happy master, topmost tot
of destiny.

BLEPYROS
                    Me?

CRIERESS
                    Indubitably, you. Who else?
Consider the staggering odds: This city contains
upwards of thirty thousand souls. Above
this mob you stand alone, both fingered by fate
and plucked by luck, the only man who's managed
to miss his dinner.

SECOND KORYPHAIA
                    Concisely and clearly put;
they don't make luck like his any more.

Sloughing the dancing girls, Blepyros
starts to the right.

CRIERESS
                                        Hold on
for a moment. Where are you off to?

BLEPYROS
                                        Where else? To dinner.

Stopping.

CRIERESS
And, thanks to Aphrodite, you'll be the last in line.
But those were your wife's instructions: To bring you along . . .

Indicating the dancing girls.

> Not to forget, of course, this brace of nymphets.
> Don't worry; there's plenty left. An excellent vintage
> from Chios. Goodies galore.

To the Chorus.

> > And don't you delay.

To the audience.

> And any of you who happen to like our play,
> —and any judges who don't let their judgment stray—,
> come on along. Provender in plenty. We're loaded.

BLEPYROS

> Don't set conditions. Extend admission to everyone
> here; no omissions. Inform them it's Liberty Hall
> for all, for grandfathers, teenagers, little kids.
> A feast awaits them, each and every one,
> assembled at startling expense . . .
> > > their own. It's time
> to go home for supper.
> > > And as for myself, I'll dash
> for dinner.

Grabbing the Crieress's torch.

> > Taking this torch along, of course.
> It's just the thing for after.

CRIERESS

> > > Why fritter away
> your time on torch songs? We want dinner music.
> You make your exit* and conduct these girls to the table;
> I'll start the meal off right with a musical potpourri.

As Blepyros, bringing the dancing girls, moves to head
the Chorus in its final dance and procession,
the First Koryphaia addresses the audience.

FIRST KORYPHAIA

> I'd like to offer the judges of the comic competition a teeny
> admonition, purely in the interests of aesthetic justice.
> > > Gentlemen:
> To the Thoughtful Judges—
> > > remember our *Message* and give us the prize.
> To the Risible Judges—
> > > remember our *Mirth* and give us the prize.
> That covers the panel. In summary, then—
> > > give us the prize.
> Also: The draw assigned our play the first production.

Don't let the four plays due to follow us* make you forget us,
but recall your oath of office and assess each chorus fairly.
Avoid the habits employed by the lesser daughters of joy
who only remember the pleasure afforded by the last man in.

CRIERESS
Uh—hey!
The milling Chorus takes no notice of her. She shouts.
AHOY!
They stop dead and turn toward her.
Ahem.
The Time has Come. So ladies, dear ladies—we know what we want;
let's do it correctly. We shall arise and go, and go
to dinner free, and go like bats out of
Crete.*
To Blepyros, as a wild, rapid music begins to sound.
—You, too.
Get those feet moving.

BLEPYROS
Just what I'm doing.

CRIERESS
Then try to convince
those empty bellies in the Chorus that they should keep up with the
dance.
It's time to taste the acme of goodness
that goes by the name of One-Dish Madness!*
*As she rapidly recites the following gibberish to a
strongly accented beat from the music, Blepyros,
his dancing girls, and the Chorus dance
madly and hungrily.*
Its hors-d'oeuvre-dotted-delicious with heart-of-the-briny oysters
and sea-tangy fishlets oh-so-zestfully nestled in clusters
on spry-as-the-morning, utterly udder-fresh goat-good cheese,
caressing a lip-smacking, tooth-tensing medley of goodies like these:
alabaster-bosomed pigeon with bee-sweet-honey-drenched thrush,
do-it-again-love dove and the brown-basted, burst-breasted gush
of thick-thighed chicken, the let-us-be-truly-thankful amen
of gobbet-good bloblets of squab, hard by the hit-me-again
of ever-so-finely-filleted, palate-proud mullet, new-speared,
with gusto-lusty sweetmeats, crunch-yummily kitcheneered
to rush the most reluctant tooth to the gnash . . .
In short, it's Heavenly
Hash.

*Pointing to someone in the audience.**

You heard the menu?
I won't detain you;
the play is almost through.
Go get a bowl . . .
then fill it with gruel;
there's nothing here for you.

BLEPYROS

The Chorus is in the throes of famine.

ENTIRE CHORUS

Then upward and onward to supper, women!

As Blepyros leads the entire company off right.

Our play may win, our play may lose;
We'll have to wait and see.
But, win or not, we eat tonight,
And that's a victory,
And that's a victory.

Exeunt omnes, cheering.

Correction. For present page number references read two digits higher: e.g., for page 7 read page 9, for page 8 read page 10, etc.

page 7. *three houses:* This is counter to the arrangement favored by most recent scholars, who opt for two houses. My preference for three is based primarily on my distribution of male parts in the first two-thirds of the play: Blepyros and Pheidolos emerge from different houses in the defecation scene; later on, Chremes has his utensils brought *out of his house* (a point often overlooked) and then confronts Pheidolos in a scene which will gain nothing but confusion if the audience presumes them to inhabit the same address. Thereafter, Houses II and III become the working residences of Hag and Crone (II) and Sweet Young Thing and Harridan (III), while House I remains Blepyros' home throughout the play, providing him with a place to entertain the dancing girls. This may appear capricious and prodigal; anyone with strong objections can certainly reblock this version for two houses. But the proposal of Miss A. M. Dale, that only one house is required, involves such strained blocking, particularly in the Epigenes episode, as to appear dramatically impractical and improbable. Not, of course, impossible—this play could be done with no set at all or with twenty houses—but hideously difficult.

7. *an invocation of the sun:* The surprise of the twist from sun to lamp gains a bit in force when it is remembered that Athenian plays were, of necessity, produced in broad daylight; but, as often, the precise relevance of the parody to the play as a whole remains a somewhat open question, not to be answered completely by invoking the comic tension produced by the contrast between expression and action. Why here, of all places? A partial answer may be found in Aristophanes' fairly consistent attempts to unsettle his audience, however slightly, at the very outset of his plays: *The Knights,* for example, begins with a scream; *The Acharnians* with a speech delivered by someone who, for the first twenty lines, appears to be a member of the audience. So here, the audience may, for some confusing moments, believe that they have wandered into a tragedy by mistake.

8. *last summer:* The Greek refers specifically to the *Skira,* a festival in honor of the goddess Athene celebrated by the women on the twelfth day of the month Skirophorion (roughly, June).

page 8. *the Congress:* The use of this term masks one important difference: The Athenian *ecclêsia* was not a representative body, but the constitutional manifestation of the Athenian people: In theory, all citizens— that is, all male citizens—over the age of twenty were qualified to take part. In practice, a quorum of 6000 was rather difficult to obtain, and payment for attendance, as noted in the Introduction, was instituted early in the fourth century B.C., one of the consequences being this play. The *ecclêsia* held stated meetings forty times during the year at the base of the Pnyx (a hill west of the Acropolis), where it deliberated and passed on legislation proposed to it by the Athenian Senate (*boulê*).

8. *those beery wenches:* According to some rather addled scholia, the name "Phyromachos" is a reference to a certain Kleomachos, possibly an actor, whose habit it was to mix up (*phyrein*) his letters. This individual once, either in a play or when proposing an action in the assembly concerning seating arrangements, pronounced the word *heteras* "others" (= other seats?) as *hetairas* "courtesans." The English approximation here employed was credited to the original Dr. Spooner.

11. *Lamios:* The translation of this desperately obscure joke, identifying Lamios as a drowsy wood-carrier and avoiding any mention of the flatulent ogress Lamia, is based on the text and interpretation given by J. Taillardat in the *Révue de philologie* 38 (1964), 38-42.

11. *a large phallos:* I have introduced this item here to point up the joke, and tie in with its undoubted appearance later. Others may prefer a carding comb.

11. *FIRST WOMAN:* Line assignments in this introductory scene vary widely and are largely arbitrary, depending on what theory is being aired. But at this point Van Leeuwen and earlier editors are clearly correct in following the Aldine edition and giving lines 102-4 to someone other than Praxagora, and my departure from Coulon's text has some precedent.

15. *on your brow:* Speakers in Athenian assemblies were wreathed. So were participants at banquets and drinking parties, a similarity which, in the Greek, prompts the Second Woman's thirst.

16. *Heavens to Betsy:* Literally, "by the Two Goddesses"—i.e., Demeter and Persephone—strictly a woman's oath. The First Woman tries again with a man's oath ("Goddam it all")—literally, "by Apollo."

18. *against the Spartans:* Presumably, the anti-Spartan coalition formed by Athens, Boiotia, Korinth, and Argos in 395, a league shortly thereafter discomfited by Spartan victories in the first year of the Korinthian War —at Nemea in July 394 and at Koronaia in August 394. "The man who'd maneuvered acceptance of the longed-for League" is identified by the scholiast as the Athenian admiral Konon.

a fighting navy: Athens was still recovering from the destruction of its fleet by the Spartans at Aigospotamoi in 405.

19. *and nobody calls:* Reading, with the Aldine edition, *horizetai* in 202. Or, to follow Coulon in adopting Hermann's *orgeizetai,* "Thrasyboulos is violently annoyed that no one calls on him." Whatever the reading, Athens' great (if touchy) hero seems to have been temporarily under a cloud. See Glossary, s. v. "Thrasyboulos."

20. *Demeter's yearly spree:* The Thesmophoria, celebrated by the women of Athens late in October.

20. *During the Terror:* Generally taken as a reference to the rule in Athens of the Thirty Tyrants in 404-403.

24. *from the countryside:* By splitting the chorus in this fashion, and indulging his usual preference for the more conservative countrymen over their urban counterparts, Aristophanes underlines the play's initial motive (the moral decay marked by the payment of congressmen) and comes nearer a conventional appeal to patriotism than at any other point in the play.

25. *PHEIDOLOS:* To William H. Hess's 1963 Princeton dissertation, *Studies in the* Ecclesiazusae *of Aristophanes,* I owe many insights into this play, plus at least one substantial improvement in its text: Hess has proved conclusively, I believe, that the initial speaker in this scene is *not* Blepyros; that lines 311-22 are delivered by another man who has been driven out-of-doors by the same nocturnal motive; that this episode, notorious already, is really a double defecation. I have not followed Hess in his development of the speaker, choosing rather, because of a certain small penuriousness in the character, to identify him with the *pheidôlos*—i.e., the "stingy man"—in the argument over the deposit of property (presumably Chremes' property) which follows Praxagora's presentation of her program.

25. *missed the head again:* While in a lyrical transport, the poet Kinesias seems to have defiled a shrine of Hekate. See *Frogs* 366.

28. *a late dispatch from the front:* In the Greek, Pheidolos replies with a question: "Would that be the plum that Thrasyboulos mentioned to the Spartans?" Concerning this plum, or rather, wild pear, the scholiast remarks: "Thrasyboulos was scheduled to speak against the Spartans who had come to see about a truce, but took a bribe instead. He then alleged that he had eaten wild pears and was too sick to speak." This seems little better than an ad hoc improvisation, though it may be true. I have preferred to develop the military imagery.

31. *the Wheat Exchange:* The Greek refers specifically to one Nausikydes, a profiteer who had made a fortune in wheat during times of war-induced shortage.

31. *dead for years:* An insertion to get some point from a joking allusion, even though a wrong one. Actually, the Nikias referred to here seems

to have been pale but still alive, the grandson of the famous Athenian general executed after the Athenian expeditionary force was annihilated in Sicily twenty-two years before.

page 39. *Great Society:* Modern analogues are the blessings and curses of the Aristophanic translator. They often provide a valuable shorthand for him and his audience, broaden and deepen references, focus satire— but they may narrow the result undesirably, import awkward side effects, drastically limit the necessarily brief life of his version. Aristophanes' point of view in this play is certainly reactionary, but to hammer the point home by translating Praxagora into Pedernalese would plug this version as hopelessly into the mid-1960's as a Paphlagonian named McKleon would strand *The Knights* in the mid-1950's. Still, one may be permitted a sidewise glance. . .

41. *until you have grasped the concept:* A number of parallels exist between Praxagora's proposals and the ideal communism—small "c"— propounded in the Fifth Book of Plato's *Republic*: community property, community of women and children, abolition of lawsuits, community feeding. Reinforced by some striking verbal parallels, these have not unnaturally engendered some burning questions, the two most important for our purposes being: (1) What was the relation of the two works? (2) What was Aristophanes' object in treating these ideas? As for question (1), I incline to the hypothesis tendered by J. L. Adam in his edition of the *Republic* (Cambridge 1902; reissued 1963): Utopian thinking was rife in Athenian intellectual circles in the last years of the fifth century and the first years of the fourth; Aristophanes adopted certain of its ideas for his play; Plato, who moved in the same circles and was writing his *Republic* at the time, was sufficiently impressed by the *Ecclesiazusae* to reply obliquely to Aristophanes' satire when, shortly after, he wrote that section of his Fifth Book which discusses the place of women and children in his Ideal State. As for question (2), Aristophanes treats this philosophical communism, not as an enemy to be annihilated, but as source material for comedy. His disapproval is undoubted, but it is not hate; he is content to pick at a few odd points, to run certain peculiarities into the ground, and then move on to the concluding banquet. The objects of his relatively good-natured satire are the Athenians so susceptible to crackpot ideas, not the ideas themselves. *The Congresswomen* is play, not pamphlet.

44. *what happens with you:* The sarcastic little exchange culminating here, implying a less than adequate home life for Praxagora and Blepyros, seems to me the only meaning that can be teased out of two lines of Greek (621-22) which editors have regularly repunctuated, rewritten, and reassigned in an effort to make them yield any sense at all. I follow Coulon's text, but assign the last four words of 622 to Blepyros.

page 45. *the flattest nose in Athens:* See Glossary, s.v. "Lysikrates."

46. *the end of your existence:* As implied earlier by his shocked reaction to his wife's putting an end to legal excesses (lines 561-62), Blepyros makes his living by informing or barratry—possibly both. I believe that his vanishing vocation is the reference here. Accordingly, I have treated lines 657b-58a as byplay between Chremes and Blepyros, inverting the order of Coulon's line assignments.

48. *the urns we used for choosing the juries:* The translation here attempts to counterfeit the humor which must have arisen from the perversion of a phenomenon very familiar to the Athenians and completely alien to moderns. In so doing, it does such violence to the Athenian legal system that I despair of correcting wrong impressions. However, there were ten principal courts in Athens. To facilitate jury assignments, each of these was designated by one of the first ten letters of the Greek alphabet. Each prospective juror drew from the *klêrôtêrion* (here translated as "urn"; really much more sophisticated than that term implies), a bronze check bearing one of those letters, then proceeded to the appropriate tribunal. In adopting this for dinner assignments, Aristophanes has added some acronymic play on locations: A check with a beta on it indicates the Basileion; one with a theta (according to the scholiast), the Theseion. Athenian topography seemed a totally impossible area for communicating humor here; I have therefore had recourse to legal *functions* . . . and have thus graced Athens with a number of separate courts which it never possessed, of which the most disturbing to me is "Delta-Divorce."

49. *FIRST WOMAN:* The distribution of this doggerel among various members of the cast has really no warrant in the Greek, which assigns the whole lot (689-709) to Praxagora. But its quasi-stanzaic structure, as developed in the translation, seemed better served by breaking it up, thus giving some employment to the otherwise mute women who have returned with Praxagora from the Pnyx—and, in Blepyros' interruptions, giving his conversion a bit more expression than the simple assent which follows.

51. *exit right:* Blepyros, when he appears again, enters from House I, and it may well be asked why we do not see him go inside it now or subsequently. The answer is quite simple: I have promoted this awkwardness to point out that it is not really an awkwardness at all. Consistency in those matters extends over very limited areas. Two pertinent points have been established about Blepyros: (1) He wishes to bask in his wife's glory . . . therefore, he leaves for the marketplace with her now; (2) he is fond of tomcatting around . . . therefore, he misses dinner while enjoying himself with the dancing girls later. These are the important considerations, the immediate motivations; others scarcely matter. It is highly unimportant, for example, whether House I remains

his home (as suggested in the first note) or is to be understood, at the play's end, as another house in another part of the city; it is primarily a place where he has been with the girls. Questions on the order of "Does his home have a back door?" belong to another sort of drama.

page 51. *CHORAL INTERLUDE:* As noted in the Introduction, the Greek here reads XOPOY—i.e., *chorou,* "the Chorus's [spot]." It is attractive to think that a complete parabasis, or at least lyrics hailing the Brave New World, might once have existed here, but nothing but naked wishing supports such a theory. A wordless dance seems as much of an *entr'acte* as it is safe to conjecture.

51. *dear sister sifter:* In setting up this well-contained equivalent of a Panathenaic procession, I have kept as close to the Greek as I could while articulating the whole by a series of bad puns. The sifter leads the procession as *arrêphoros* "basket-bearer"—the Maid of Honor who carried the goddess Athene's sacred relics. A pot follows as *diphrophoros* "bench-bearer" to the leader. The lady-in-waiting is unspecified, but Aristophanes employed a water clock in *The Wasps,* and might as well again. Likewise, a pitcher seems a logical pitcher-bearer. The trouble comes with the addition of music—what is to represent the *kitharôidos,* the lyre-player (here transmitted into "the band")? Something which makes a sound in the mornings . . . but the text does not specify. The scholiast points the way toward a handmill; Rogers imported a rooster (rather illogically, given the nature of its companions, though there is one in *The Wasps*); rather deplorably, I opt for the *skôramis,* the chamber pot, already present in the play's fabric through its mention in the defecation scene. Its megaphonic qualities are well known, and, as a way of getting one out of bed, it seems unrivaled.

58. *ceiling on salt:* Evidently, a recent attempt at price control which, the scholiast notes, was passed by the Congress but never put into effect.

58. *when silver was short:* The Spartan occupation of Attika in the later years of the Peloponnesian War shut Athens off from her silver mines at Laurion, forcing a famous if short-lived issue of copper coinage in 406. See *Frogs* 725.

59. *Euripides' bill:* The Euripides mentioned here is not the tragic poet; the date of his attempted direct levy on the citizenry, never executed, is unknown.

59. *Waitresses:* Actually, perfume-girls (*myropôlides*), whose function would be to supply and, possibly, anoint the banqueters with scented oils.

62. *Now, what:* Most editors supply the solution to Pheidolos' problem entirely within the text itself, translating the next two lines (875-76) in some such way as this: "I see precisely what to do [*viz.*]: I have to go along with them to dinner, and not delay." No props are employed; Pheidolos' subtle contrivance, his *mêchanêma,* his gimmick for sharing

food with Chremes and the rest is . . . to go to dinner with them. Given that this is precisely what he is trying to find a way to do, we have the whole scene conclude on the flattest nonjoke in Aristophanes. [Van Leeuwen felt the difficulty and tried to beef up the context by stating that Pheidolos obviously intended to fight his way in. This is (a) not obvious and (b) not much help.] I do not claim truth for what must seem the overuse of my already hypothetical chamber pot, but it does have certain advantages: It supplies Pheidolos with his wished-for gimmick in previously defined terms (a container to carry in the dinner procession); its purpose is clear to the audience; and, in a chamber pot's buying one's way to food, it possesses a certain irony which, however small, is funnier than going to dinner by going to dinner. (I repunctuate the Greek in 875 as follows: half stop or full stop after *orthôs* and a full stop instead of a half stop after *phainetai*.)

page 63. *a large leather phallos:* The precise item indicated by the Hag has been a matter of conjecture for a good many centuries. The dildo seems the best of a number of rather greasy possibilities, if only because its presence is definitely required late in the subsequent exchange of songs . . . where the Greek refers to it (though my English does not) by the proper name "Orthagoras"—i.e., "Mr. Hardon."

64. *to the same tune:* In the Hag's response here, with her echoes of the Sweet Young Thing, I follow the text of 918 ff. as reconstructed by John Jackson (*Marginalia Scaenica,* 109-10). The reassignment of the lines—that is, the shift back to the Sweet Young Thing at 922—is my own.

64. *to put the L in Lesbos:* This rendering, where obscenity is reinforced by obscurity, seems fairly close to the effect of the Greek at 920: "You look to me like a *lambda,* as they say in Lesbos"—or, less likely, "You seem ready to *lambda* in the Lesbian fashion." The scholiast helpfully points out that lambda is the first letter of *leichazein* "lick." Unfairly or not, the island of Lesbos' persistent reputation as a hotbed of female homosexuality arose as a reaction to the life and works of the poetess Sappho.

65. *eaten by moths years back:* To the name Epigenes, "late-born," the Sweet Young Thing counters with *Gerês*—i.e., "Antique." Since the rendering of puns on proper names usually results in Greeks with Anglo-Saxon names, I have tried to work around the problem.—But is the young man's name really Epigenes? When he appears, the mss give *neos* "young (male)"; Coulon follows Brunck and indicates him by *neanias* "young man"; he is never again referred to by name in the text. I have stuck with "Epigenes" to gain a wee bit of particularization; in this play, a named character is worth rubies.

66. *a rather vapid love duet:* This song may be our earliest full example of a noble minor genre, the *paraklausithyron*—the song to be sung by a

frustrated lover before his mistress's closed door—but that is no reason to treat it with reverence. Aristophanes is here parodying pop lyrics, with their reliance on threadbare refrains and their debasement of high-falutin language, and the effect aimed for is bathos. See C. M. Bowra, "A Love-Duet," *American Journal of Philology*, 79 (1958), 376-91.

page 68. *to deliver a warrant:* The original turns on proper-name puns. Epigenes, flustered, pretends a search for a man from the Athenian deme of Anaphlystos (pun on *anaphlan* "masturbate") whose name is not Sebinos (pun on *binein* "screw"). In their stead, I have inserted the warrant-subpoena bit, which should supply the requisite double entendres and at the same time segue logically into the remarks on the crowded court calendar.

71. *The still-life man:* The English here evokes undertaking; the Greek— "the man who paints the *lekythoi* for the dead"—reaches its goal by a different route. These graceful oil bottles, decorated with white-figured paintings, stood at the head of the body while it lay in state and were then buried with it. The painter might have wanted the Hag as prospective user or, more intriguingly, as model for the dead-white figures.

72. *The use tax:* "Sales Tax" might be closer. The reference here seems to be to a fairly recent two-mil impost on all exchanges of property.

73. *hitting below the belt:* In the Greek, Epigenes declares (somewhat illogically, but it's to be expected) that he'll become Prokroustes, or Procrustes—the legendary bandit with the terribly strange bed who stretched or cut his guests to fit it—punning on the sexual sense of *prokrouein* "beat" or "bang."

73. *than he can raise on the spot:* The Greek is more specific and less sexual: "No man's good for more than a bushel now." Under Athenian law, a woman could only make a contract where the value at stake was less than a bushel (*medimnos*) of wheat; the Hag is serving notice, if any were needed, that the tables are turned.

73. *are one and the same:* In the Greek, the Hag informs Epigenes that it is a "Diomedeian necessity" for him to accompany her. This phrase, proverbial for "ineluctable necessity," is of uncertain origin, though it probably refers to Diomedes or Diomede, one of the Greek heroes in the *Iliad*. The scholium here, evidently written by a euhemerist who was trying to explain (1) the proverb, (2) its use in this particular context, and (3) the legend of the man-eating horses of the bandit Diomedes of Thrace (the object of Herakles' Eighth Labor), is clearly wrong, but has its own insane charm: "The Thracian Diomedes' daughters were whores. When strangers came his way, he forced them to make love to his daughters until the girls were satisfied and the men died of exhaustion. The legend called these girls his man-eating horses." With the aim of avoiding this mares' nest, the translation deforms one

of the best-known lines of the philosopher Herakleitos, to whom apologies are due.

page 74. *black wax:* The color is gratuitous misinformation by the translator to reinforce the (possibly incorrect) impression given by the Greek of the existence of such items as waxen funeral wreaths. Conceivably, what is involved is a pun on *kêrinôn* "waxen" and *Kêr* "Death."

74. *an Oedipus complex:* Not nearly the anachronism it might seem. "Carry out that law," goes the Greek, "and you'll fill the country full of Oedipusses."

80. *CHORAL INTERLUDE:* The mss give no indication of it, but some choral action seems probable at this point, and so I follow Bergk and Blaydes in reading XOPOY here.

80. *Crieress:* The character who now appears is feminine and a servant to a woman of some importance. Thus, the mss have named her "Therapaina"—"Maidservant," relating her not at all to any previous character. They are followed by all editors, and I think wrongly. This clearly should be the Crieress, the She-Herald who has appeared before, interrupting the argument between Chremes and Pheidolos to invite the men to dinner. (There, incidentally, since she does not disclose her sex in her announcement, the mss refer to her by the masculine noun *Kêryx* "Herald.") To move even further back, it seems obvious, though unprovable, that the existence of this character, a female Herald who is the servant or functionary of Praxagora, was set up by the Commistress-in-Chief herself, shortly before her final exit, when, at line 713 (p. 50) she noted that she had to procure a Crieress (*kêrykaina*), a "girl with a nice shrill voice to handle public announcements." The difference between the Crieress's mode of speech at her former appearance and now is simply explained: She has been at the banquet and is drunk. Though this may seem a problematical change, it marks the progression of time and gaiety, and provides the play with some sorely needed continuity. It is some comfort in this regard that most scholars persist in considering her Praxagora's servant, and thus identify the tardy husband as Blepyros.

82. *You make your exit:* Those who hold that Aristophanes' theater possessed a platform stage above and distinct from the Chorus' dancing area, the *orchêstra*, may prefer the translation: "You come down [i.e., from stage to orchestra]." But the verb here employed, *katabainein* "descend," is the standard term for "exit"; in leaving the playing area of Athens' Theater of Dionysos, one *descends* by the *parodoi*—its nearest equivalent to wing exits.

83. *the four plays due to follow us:* Early in the fourth century, the number of plays entered in the comic contests at each Athenian dramatic festival was increased from three to five. I have incorporated this intelligence to give the passage here more point, though it may be

inaccurate; records are lacking for 392, the probable year of *The Congresswomen*'s production. The earliest year for which this innovation is noted is 388, when Aristophanes entered his *Ploutos* against Nikochares' *Laconians,* Aristomenes' *Admetos,* Nikophon's *Adonis,* and Alkaios' *Pasiphae.*

page 83. *like bats out of Crete:* In the Greek, instruction is given to dance *krêtikôs* "in the Cretan (or cretic) manner." This is usually interpreted: (1) as a reference to a type of dance, accompanied by music and pantomime, which originated on Crete; or (2) as a rhythmical indication, where the metrical unit specified might not be the usual cretic (— ∪ —), but the so-called "cretic of Aristoxenos," the ditrochee (— ∪ — ∪).

83. *One-Dish Madness:* The dozen lines which follow are an attempt to provide in English something like the effect of the longest word in the Greek language, an original coinage which Aristophanes formed by jamming the names of two dozen items of food into a monstrous compound noun, a melange which reproduces linguistically the hash it describes. Running to seven lines, it looks, in transliteration from Coulon's text, like this:

> *lepadotemachoselachogaleo-*
> *kranioleipsanodrimypotrimmato-*
> *silphiotyromelitokatakechymeno-*
> *kichlepikossyphophattoperistera-*
> *lektryonoptokephaliokinklope-*
> *leiolagôiosiraiobaphêtraga-*
> *lopterygôn.*

Greek's affinity for compounds has been run into the ground, definitively, perhaps in parody of the poet Philoxenos of Leukas, whose gourmet dithyramb, *The Banquet,* abounded in lesser specimens of the art. Unhappily for the translator into English, his language will not agglutinate like Greek or German; a string of English nouns, however connected, remains a string of nouns. I have therefore had recourse to an analogue which is, blessedly, adaptable to food: The building of insane compound premodifiers which so fascinates the advertising industry as it carries out its quickening work.

84. *to someone in the audience:* The Crieress is carrying out Blepyros' instructions and depriving the audience of the huge morsel so lovingly described above. This Indian-giving vis-a-vis the spectators appears to have been a common comic bit, especially toward a play's end (e.g., *Lysistrata* 1043-71, 1189-1215), and should be accorded no especial significance here. Wilamowitz, however, wanted bitterness, and posited Blepyros as the addressee of these verses; the Brave New World thus concludes by cheating the principal male character of his dinner. Eduard Fraenkel went even further in curdling the cream of the jest;

for Blepyros in this scene, he substituted the "dutiful man" (Chremes in this version), whom he chose to describe as the *only* man who had carried out the new directives, and proceeded to cheat *him* of his dinner. Such attempts, however ingenious, are misplaced; they try to pervert an extravaganza into an anticommunist tract by an ill-motivated, unindicated last-minute twist which goes counter to the whole tenor of the text. (As for the use of the singular in an address to the audience, see *Acharnians* 836 ff.)

Glossary

AGYRRHIOS: Athenian demagogue; radical-democrat politician who reached the height of his power and influence in the middle and late 390's, following his introduction of a one-obol wage for assembly attendance and subsequent increase of the rate to three obols. His position as head of the war party did not guarantee him military achievement, however; he succeeded Thrasyboulos as head of the Athenian fleet on the latter's death at Lesbos in 388, but was replaced shortly thereafter. Subsequently, he went to prison for embezzlement. His appearance was evidently effeminate enough to cause comic comment, but Aristophanes may hardly have been unprejudiced: Agyrrhios seems to have been responsible for cutting the pay of comic poets shortly before 405.

AMYNON: A homosexual orator; a pathic.

ANTILOCHOS: Son of Nestor; one of the Greek heroes in the Trojan War, where (Iliad 18.18) he brought Achilles the news of the death of his friend Patroklos.

ANTISTHENES: An extremely wealthy homosexual, very effeminate in appearance.

APHRODITE: Goddess of beauty and sexual love.

APOLLO: God of prophecy, music, healing, and light.

ARIPHRADES: Son of Automenes and a notorious pervert. The creative nature of his perversities (cunnilingual and worse) kept him a standard object of Aristophanic satire for more than thirty years.

ARISTYLLOS: A homosexual of peculiarly disgusting habits. Once identified by the nineteenth-century scholar Bergk, on little better than no evidence at all, as the philosopher Plato. This piece of ingenuity found scarcely any acceptance, and Bergk seems to have thought better of it.

ATHENE: Goddess of wisdom and war; patron of Athens.

CHIOS: Island in the central Aegean, famous for its wine.

CRETE: A large Greek island in the Mediterranean, southeast of the Greek mainland.

DEMETER: The Earth-Mother; goddess of grain, agriculture, and the harvest.

EPIGONOS: A strikingly effeminate Athenian.

EPIKOUROS: A pervert.

EPIKRATES: A hairy politician, whose beard was so bushy that he was called *sakesphoros* "strainer-bearer"; a member of the war party at Athens; once accused of taking bribes while on an embassy to Persia.

EUAION: A most eloquent deadbeat—which is all we can gain from text and scholia. W. H. Hess would identify him with the exceptionally strong brother of Leodamas the Acharnian, mentioned decades later by the orator Demosthenes.

EURIPIDES: (1) Athenian tragedian (480-406 B.C.), whose plays were constantly ridiculed and parodied by Aristophanes. (2) A politician considerably younger than (1)—some conjecture his son—who proposed an unsuccessful levy not too long before 392.

HARMODIOS: Athenian hero who, with Aristogeiton, assassinated the tyrant Hipparchos in 514 and was put to death. Statues to Harmodios and Aristogeiton were erected in the Athenian Agora.

HERAKLES: Hero and demigod, son of Zeus and Alkmene, renowned for his great labors, his prodigious strength, and his gluttonous appetite. The point of his invocation by Epigenes at the sight of the Harridan seems to be partly informational; his twelfth labor took him to the underworld to bring back the three-headed dog Kerberos.

KALLIAS: Son of Hipponikos; a notorious profligate and spendthrift who had run through a fortune.

KALLIMACHOS: An extremely impecunious dramatic poet.

KASTOR: Divinity, son of Leda and Tyndaros, or of Leda and Zeus; twin of Polydeukes (Pollux), with whom he constitutes the Dioskouroi, helpers of men in distress.

KEPHALOS: Son of a potter; a rigidly constitutional democratic politician. A member of the war party, he was instrumental in urging Athens to abandon neutrality in 394 and combine with other Greek states against Sparta.

KINESIAS: A dithyrambic poet with curious ideas of personal hygiene.

KORINTH: A Greek city situated at the narrowest point of the isthmus which bears its name, the neck of land which joins the Peloponneses to the rest of mainland Greece. It was this strategic location which led to constant attacks by invading Spartans in the later 390's and gave the Corinthian War (394-386) its name.

LEUKOLOPHOS: A pervert.

LYSIKRATES: A dark, effeminate, snub-nosed, aging roué who took to dyeing his hair to appear younger.

MYRONIDES: Athenian general of the mid-fifth century. His best-known victory was over the Boiotians at Oinophyta (456). A stock symbol, for Aristophanes, of the Good Old Days when Men were Men and Virtue was Untarnished.

NEOKLEIDES: A blear-eyed politician generally satirized for his ailment, for light-fingeredness, and for alien birth. W. H. Hess theorizes that Aristophanes may use this name to attack Herakleides of Klazomenai, a naturalized alien who was responsible for increasing the legislative pay instituted by Agyrrhios from one obol to three obols. If so, Aristophanes (who attacks "Neokleides" twice in this play and three times in the *Ploutos*) and other poets are untypically coy in avoiding an enemy's real name; but the theory is an attractive one.

NIKIAS: A pale young man, probably the grandson of the ill-fated Athenian general.

PAN: Rural Arkadian god of the flocks and woodlands; associated with sudden madness (hence "panic"). His cult at Athens was instituted by way of thanks for his help to the Athenians at the battle of Marathon.

PHYROMACHOS: According to the scholiast, this name masks Kleomachos, an actor or an orator (or possibly both) with deplorable diction.

POLLUX: Twin of Kastor (q.v.).

POSEIDON: Brother of Zeus and god of the sea.

SMOIOS: A notorious pervert, whose interests seem to have run in the same channels as those of Ariphrades (q.v.).

SPARTA: Capital city of Lakonia, Athens' principal opponent and conqueror in the Peloponnesian War; at this time (392) the greatest single power in Greece, and thus engaged in war against a coalition of lesser Greek powers (Athens, Korinth, Argos, Thebes) while carrying on a naval conflict against Persia.

THASOS: A volcanic island in the northern Aegean, celebrated for the dark, fragrant wine produced by its vineyards.

THRASYBOULOS: Athenian hero, deliverer of the city from the rule of the Thirty Tyrants in 404 B.C. Thereafter, he pursued a moderate course politically, being outmaneuvered by the radical-democratic war party on Athens' entrance into the Corinthian War in 394. Regained much of Athens' northern dominions in 390-389; killed at Lesbos in 388.

ZEUS: Chief god of the Olympian pantheon: son of Kronos, brother of Poseidon, father of Athene.